THE NON-PROPHET'S GUIDE TO THE END TIMES

Written & Illustrated by

ToDD HAMPSON

HARVEST HOUSE PUBLISHERS
EUGENE, OREGON

Cover art © by Todd Hampson

Cover by Left Coast Design

Published in association with William K. Jensen Literary Agency, 119 Bampton Court, Eugene, Oregon 97404.

Dedicated to my wife Tracey—the love of my life,
and our children—Daniel, Natalie, and Luke.
Your encouragement helped this book to become a reality.
I love you all beyond measure.

The Non-Prophet's Guide™ to the End Times

Copyright © 2018—text © by Todd Hampson; artwork © by Todd Hampson
Published by Harvest House Publishers
Eugene, Oregon 97408
www.harvesthousepublishers.com

ISBN 978-0-7369-7279-6 (pbk.)
ISBN 978-0-7369-7280-2 (eBook)

Library of Congress Cataloging-in-Publication Data
Names: Hampson, Todd, author.
Title: The non-prophet's guide to the end times / Todd Hampson.
Description: Eugene : Harvest House Publishers, 2018.
Identifiers: LCCN 2018006864 (print) | LCCN 2018016430 (ebook) | ISBN
   9780736972802 (ebook) | ISBN 9780736972796 (pbk.)
Subjects: LCSH: Bible—Prophecies. | End of the world—Biblical teaching.
Classification: LCC BS647.3 (ebook) | LCC BS647.3 .H36 2018 (print) | DDC
   220.1/5—dc23
LC record available at https://lccn.loc.gov/2018006864

Printed in the United States of America

21 22 23 24 25 26 / VP-JC / 10 9 8

CONTENTS

PART 4: So Where Are We Now?

PART 1:

THE DEFINITION, NATURE, AND IMPORTANCE OF BIBLE PROPHECY

CHAPTER 1

What Is Bible Prophecy, and Why Is It So Important?

"Men of Galilee," they said, "why do you stand here looking into the sky? This same Jesus, who has been taken from you into heaven, will come back in the same way you have seen him go into heaven."

ACTS 1:11

Have you ever really thought about the truth contained in this verse or in many others like it? If the idea of Christ's return has become overly familiar to you, read that verse again and let it sink in as if you had never read it before. Scripture tells us Jesus is literally coming back to earth one day. Are you aware of how frequently the writers of the New Testament wrote about the promised return of Christ? Of the 27 books in the New Testament, 23 mention his return. Jesus often spoke about it himself. In the 66 books of the Bible, you'll find that one out of every 30 verses refers to the return of Christ or the topic of the end times. So it's fair to say this is a major biblical theme from cover to cover.

Down through the centuries, Jesus's followers have fully believed, taught, and expected that he would return. During the past 2,000 years of church history, core Christian beliefs have been codified into simple statements of faith called creeds. These concise statements affirm that the return of

27-33%
PROPHECY

10,000+
VERSES

50%
FULFILLED

50%
FUTURE

7

Christ has always been a key focus of the Christian faith. This truth has brought encouragement to generations of Christians who have looked to a promised future where all things will be made right. We are reminded of this promise every time we take communion and "proclaim the Lord's death until he comes" (1 Corinthians 11:26). We also pray for the arrival of the end times in the Lord's prayer whenever we pray, "Your kingdom come, your will be done, on earth as it is in heaven" (Matthew 6:10).

However, in recent decades, the topic of Christ's return has, for various reasons, taken a bad rap. What comes to mind when you read these words? *Revelation. Apocalypse. Armageddon. End times. The last days. Judgment.* If images of a bullhorn-wielding sidewalk preacher donned in a sandwich board comes to mind, you are not alone.

Unfortunately the topic of Christ's return has been hijacked by caricatured notions of what the Bible actually teaches. It's not a doom-and-gloom scare tactic. His return is a foundational truth of the Christian faith, but in our day, we tend to treat the topic like a crazy uncle the family never talks about.

In conversations with fellow believers, I find that most of them truly believe the Lord is going to return at some point, but they see this as a distant event with no real relevance for us today. Many are confused about the last days or they completely ignore the topic. This is understandable for many reasons, but I hope to demonstrate through this book that studying eschatology and Bible prophecy is a thousand times more relevant and practical than many Christians realize.

Revelation 1:3—Blessed is the one who reads aloud the words of this prophecy, and blessed are those who hear it and take to heart what is written in it, because the time is near.

Revelation 1:3 boldly states, "Blessed is the one who reads aloud the words of this prophecy, and blessed are those who hear it and take to heart what is written in it, because the time is near." So the final book of the Bible, which many believers in our day tend to avoid, informs us that there are specific blessings for those who read it!

Some of the confusion and apathy about end-times events is caused by the fact there are multiple views, interpretive disagreements, and case after case of failed predictions about when Christ would return—a practice that violates Scripture. Matthew 24:36 says, "About that day or hour no one knows, not even the angels in heaven, nor the Son, but only the Father." That's about as clear as Jesus could get, yet it seems there is an endless parade of people picking dates for Christ's return. This does unnecessary harm to the Christian faith. One of the main goals of this book is to address this confusion and to demonstrate that not only can Revelation and other prophetic texts be understood, but that by studying them your faith will grow and your relationship with Jesus will deepen.

There's another reason I wrote this book. The world is a scary place right now, and many people are wondering what is going on. There has always been instability, but never on the global scale that we see in our day. It seems like the world is going to hell in a handbasket. I don't know exactly what a handbasket is, but the term seems to fit.

Consider this list of some of the unprecedented conditions of our day:

- terrorism on almost every continent
- global refugee crisis
- international financial instability
- division in America

- Ebola, Zika, superbugs, and other diseases
- one record-breaking natural disaster after another
- citizens killing cops, and cops killing citizens
- racial tensions
- widespread genocide
- mass shootings
- civil wars and uprisings
- unparalleled persecution of Christians
- people selling baby parts while society yawns
- dangerous countries getting nukes
- ever-increasing immorality and family breakdown
- occultism and unprecedented hedonism on display by our pop-culture icons
- cyberwarfare
- political corruption and distrust at an all-time high
- the decline of America

Aren't you glad you read that list? Read on. I promise it will get more encouraging.

Is this just the way things are, or are these signals that history is drawing to a close? Suddenly, the notion isn't that crazy. Even secular futurologists are sounding the alarms as they see converging lines of danger and instability around the world. TV shows and movies with apocalyptic themes abound. These trends are clearly on the minds of everyone who has turned on the news the past few years. It's time to talk about this elephant in the room.

POP-CULTURE MEDIA TRENDS

957 "APOCALYPTIC" MOVIES
67% of those since 2000

88 "APOCALYPTIC" TV SHOWS
66% of those since 2000 (Source: IMDB.com)

So, should we buy space in a luxury underground community bunker? I'm not joking; they're actually out there. Should we begin stocking up on food, ammo, and medicine? Or should we live with boldness, hope, joy, expectation, and confidence in a soon-coming King? Can the Bible shed light on what we are witnessing in the world today and provide clear marching orders?

This book will answer those endtime questions and more. My goal is to make complex things simple and move you from a state of ambiguity and confusion to one of courage and clarity. After you read this book, my hope is that you will walk away with a firm understanding of key end-time events, see that the book of Revelation can be clearly understood, and be able to recognize the biblical signs that help us understand our times.

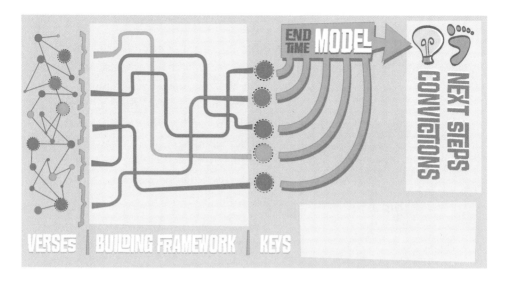

VERSES | BUILDING FRAMEWORK | KEYS

Answers to Basic Questions About Bible Prophecy

Using the analogy of building a house, let's start the work of laying the foundation by answering some basic but very important questions.

1. What is Bible prophecy?

Simply put, Bible prophecy is God revealing history in advance. Prophecies are divinely inspired revelations given by God through a person. Prophecies were given as predictions, warnings, or directives for taking action. In the New Testament, Peter tells us how prophecies were given:

> Above all, you must understand that no prophecy of Scripture came about by the prophet's own interpretation of things. For prophecy never had its origin in the human will, but prophets, though

human, spoke from God as they were carried along by the Holy Spirit (2 Peter 1:20-21).

The technical term for the study of end-time Bible prophecy events is *eschatology*. Eschatology means "the study of last things." *Merriam-Webster's Dictionary* defines it as "a branch of theology concerned with the final events in the history of the world or of humankind." Eschatology touches on all other key areas of systematic biblical study.

Genesis, the first book of the Bible, introduces key themes that are progressively revealed in later books, and these themes find their final resolution in Revelation—the last and distinctively prophetic book of the Bible. The Bible, though written by at least 39 men on three continents over a period of at least 1,500 years, tells one complete story beginning with eternity past and ending with eternity future.

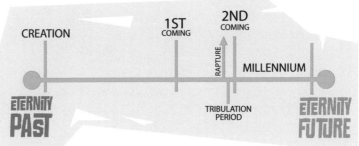

Unlike the vague predictions of modern-day psychics and palm readers, Bible prophecies are specific predictions of future events given through God's appointed prophets. The main test of a true prophet is that their predictions must come true 100 percent of the time.

> If what a prophet proclaims in the name of the LORD does not take place or come true, that is a message the LORD has not spoken. The prophet has spoken presumptuously, so do not be alarmed (Deuteronomy 18:22).

Another important test of a prophet is that their prophecies must agree with Scripture and not cause anyone to worship false gods.

> If a prophet, or one who foretells by dreams, appears among you and announces to you a sign or wonder, and if the sign or wonder spoken of takes place, and the prophet says, "Let us follow other gods" (gods you have not known) "and let us worship them," you must not listen to the words of that prophet or dreamer. The LORD your God is testing you to find out whether you love him with all your heart and with all your soul. It is the LORD your God you must follow, and him you must revere. Keep his commands and obey him; serve him and hold fast to him (Deuteronomy 13:1-4).

Another important aspect of prophecy is that it displays the character and nature of God. Through the prophets, God made it clear that only he can appoint and predict future events. In essence, God ties his own credibility and character to the accuracy of Bible prophecy.

> I am the LORD; that is my name! I will not give my glory to anyone else, nor share my praise with carved idols. Everything I prophesied has come true, and now I will prophesy again. I will tell you the future before it happens (Isaiah 42:8-9 NLT).

sov•er•eign = God is in control
adjective

om•nis•cient = God is actually the only
adjective   true "know-it-all"

2. Why is Bible prophecy important for you?

Here's why Bible prophecy is important for you. Fulfilled Bible prophecy is one of the most compelling evidences that the Bible is from God. As you will discover in this book, major historical events were told centuries, and in some cases, thousands of years in advance. These prophecies were fulfilled to the exact detail. No other document in the world can make this claim. The only logical explanation is that the book is supernatural in nature.

WORLD EVENTS PROPHESIED IN SCRIPTURE

FOUR EMPIRES: BABYLON, MEDO-PERSIA, GREECE, ROME	DANIEL CH. 2, 7
DESTRUCTION OF THE CITY OF TYRE	EZEKIEL 26
DESTRUCTION OF THE CITY OF SIDON	EZEKIEL 28
PERSIAN KING CYRUS PROPHESIED BY NAME	ISAIAH 44:28
JEWISH PEOPLE WOULD BE DISPERSED 2X'S	ISAIAH 11:11
ISRAEL WOULD BE REBORN IN A DAY AFTER A LONG TIME	ISAIAH 66:8
KNOWLEDGE AND TRAVEL WOULD GREATLY INCREASE	DANIEL 12:4
WORLD WAR	MATTHEW 24

I can't show God to you, but I can show you his fingerprints all over fulfilled prophecy. I would encourage you to read this book with an attitude of genuine truth-seeking wherever it may lead. Christianity is believed by faith, but I hope to demonstrate to you that it is a faith built on facts and evidence rather than a blind faith. God never expected us to check our brains at the door as we consider the claims of Scripture. For those sincerely seeking patterns of evidence, I believe these patterns will lead you to the God of the Bible.

Fulfilled Bible prophecy also demonstrates God's faithfulness. He is a promise-keeper. One expert states, "It is a well-known fact among prophecy scholars that there were more than one thousand prophecies contained within the Bible at the time that it was written, and over five hundred of these have been fulfilled. The remainder are end-time prophecies whose time has not yet come."[1]

1000+ PROPHECIES 500 ALREADY FULFILLED

Experts report that 27-33 percent of the Bible is prophecy. More than 10,000 of the 31,102 verses in the Bible contain prophecy, and half of those have already been fulfilled. That is no small down payment. God has put his money where his mouth is and demonstrated his promise-keeping faithfulness to generations of believers.

End-time prophecies predict several breathtaking events, not the least of which is the rapture, in which all true believers in Christ will be taken to be with the Lord in an instant prior to a terrible time on Earth known as the tribulation. If not for the avalanche of already-fulfilled prophecies, it would be extremely difficult to believe some of the amazing claims of end-time prophecies.

QUICK FACTS: ABOUT THE RAPTURE

First Corinthians 15:51-53 and 1 Thessalonians 4:16-17 are the primary texts describing the rapture. The term "rapture" comes from the Latin word "rapturo," which is a translation of the Greek verb "caught up" that is found in 1 Thessalonians 4:17. Calling it "the rapture" is a bit easier than calling it "the caught up."

Last but not least, Bible prophecy should motivate us to share the good news about God's free gift of salvation with our friends and loved ones. Whether we'll see the Lord return in our day or not, we are closer to those events than any other generation in history. Furthermore, we are witnessing a convergence of end-time conditions which, at the very least, demonstrate that the world is being readied for end-time prophecies to be fulfilled. As one prophecy expert often says, "Things are not falling apart, they are falling into place!"

Even if the Lord does not return in our lifetime, we all need to be ready to meet him at death. When my mother died a few years ago, the suddenness of her sickness and death took me by surprise. It also reminded me that we are not guaranteed tomorrow. In Christ, we have the answer to everything, and we need to share that!

Romans 1:16—For I am not ashamed of the gospel, because it is the power of God that brings salvation to everyone who believes.

3. What are the end-time signs?

When you hear people refer to end-time signs, they are generally talking about one of two things. First, they may be referring to specific signs the Bible tells us to look for that signal the nearness of Christ's return. Second, they may be talking about specific world conditions forming in our day that mirror the conditions described in Bible prophecy. These conditions are logically necessary for key events to occur during the seven-year tribulation mentioned above.

We will cover both categories and list specific signs in later chapters. For now I want to define what a legitimate end-time sign is. I also want to show that attempting to understand our time is approved and encouraged in Scripture. We are told in 1 Chronicles 12:32 that the leaders of Issachar "understood the signs of the times and knew the best course for Israel to take" (NLT). The wise men from the East (Matthew 2:1-2), the godly old man Simeon (Luke 2:25-35), and the old prophetess Anna (Luke 2:36-38) all understood the time frame of the Lord's first arrival, and their amazing stories are recorded for us in Scripture.

QUICK FACT: DID YOU KNOW...
the wise men from the East were linked to ancient Babylon, where the prophet Daniel was in captivity and gave time-specific prophecies of the coming Messiah?

WISE MEN! NOT WISE GUYS! AND, NO...THEY WEREN'T IN THE MAFIA OR FROM NEW YORK!

BUT THE VERSE SAYS THEY CAME FROM THE EAST.

SERIOUSLY?

We also find that Jesus rebuked the Pharisees and the crowds of people for not knowing the signs of their day. To the scribes and Pharisees he said, "You know how to interpret the weather signs in the sky, but you don't know how to interpret the signs of the times!" (Matthew 16:3 NLT). To the crowds he said, "You fools! You know how to interpret the weather signs of the earth and sky, but you don't know how to interpret the present times" (Luke 12:56 NLT).

In what is known as the Olivet Discourse, Jesus responded to a question asked by his disciples. After informing them that the beautiful temple and surrounding buildings they were admiring would be completely destroyed, the disciples asked Jesus a critical three-part question.

THIS WAS FULFILLED 37 YEARS LATER BY THE ROMANS IN A.D. 70

"As Jesus was sitting on the Mount of Olives, the disciples came to him privately. 'Tell us,' they said, 'when will this happen, and what will be the sign of your coming and of the end of the age?'" (Matthew 24:3).

Rather than rebuke them or downplay the question, Jesus gave them a full chapter's worth of signs followed by another full chapter of related parables. This central teaching by Jesus regarding the end-time signs is recorded in three of the four Gospels—in Matthew 24, Luke 21, and Mark 13.

THE "OLIVET DISCOURSE" IS A FANCY WAY OF SAYING, "the talk Jesus had with his disciples on the mountain ridge with the olive trees on it just east of Jerusalem."

The apostle Paul, whom God used to take Christianity to the Gentiles, realized that the church age was the last age or era before the rapture and the terrible tribulation period. He tells us in Romans 13:11-12, "This is all the more urgent, for you know how late it is; time is running out. Wake up, for our salvation is nearer now than when we first believed. The night is almost gone; the day of salvation will soon be here." If this was true in Paul's day, it's even truer today, since almost 2,000 years have passed.

Finally, the writer of Hebrews provides the insight that those who are alive close to the time of Jesus's return will be able to recognize that they are in the season of the Lord's coming. Consider the bold statement in the latter part of this verse: "...not giving up meeting together, as some are in the habit of doing, but encouraging one another—and all the more as you see the Day approaching" (Hebrews 10:25).

The Main Reason for Prophecy

"The essence of prophecy is to give a clear witness for Jesus" (Revelation 19:10 NLT).

Studying Bible prophecy and understanding our times is one of the most fascinating and faith-building adventures we can take. The verse above informs us that the main purpose of prophecy is to give us a clear portrait of Jesus. He came the first time as a suffering servant and paid for our sins with his life. He rose from the grave and defeated death and evil. One day soon he is coming back as a conquering King to claim that victory in all of its fullness. Studying Bible prophecy points us to these amazing events and gives us hope, direction, purpose, and strength in a scary and confusing time.

Now that we have laid a basic foundation by clarifying what Bible prophecy is and why it's important to every believer, including you, let's start building our metaphorical house as we define some key end-time terms and unpack the four main views Christians hold to about the last days.

CHAPTER 2

How Does Prophecy Prove Divine Authorship?

I am God, and there is none like me.
I make known the end from the beginning,
from ancient times, what is still to come.

ISAIAH 46:9-10

A few years ago I worked with a team that developed an animated show concept for tweens called *Guardian High*. The storyline had to do with a group of teens from different time periods who were brought together in the twenty-first century, where they attract the attention of an ancient evil enemy who threatens to destroy time itself. The chronologically diverse teens have to work together to prevent the destruction of time, learn how to fit into twenty-first-century America, and turn their homework in on time.

While developing the show concept, we had to research the nature of time and the nature of light. We had no idea what mind-bending facts awaited us in our research path in order to make our story cohesive and entertaining. One of the parameters we looked at closely was how we as people are bound by the constraints of time, but God is not. We're "stuck" in time, which we experience linearly, but God by his very nature is outside of time. He created it; therefore, he transcends it. To God, time is more like an object than a chronological experience.

Here's one way to think of it. God views time a bit like we would view a river from a helicopter. The river is constantly moving downstream from point A to point B, but in the helicopter, we are able to move back and forth to different locations along the river and we can increase our altitude so that we can view the entire river all at once. With a simple turn of the head, we can see different points on the river that are miles apart.

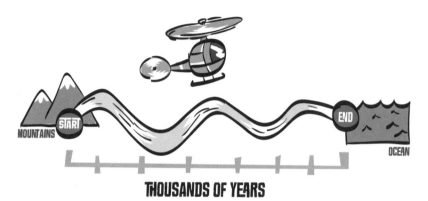

Prophecy is simply God's description of history before it happens. God sees any point of time at will, so looking into the future is not a big deal for him. He can look through the hallways of both eternity past and eternity future. His panoramic simultaneous view of all things is a mystery to us because we are his finite creation, and the infinite Creator does not fit neatly into the space between our ears.

Logic and the Bible

If we believe God created time, it's not at all a stretch to suggest that God can predict the future with complete accuracy. If that's the case, it gives us a chance to test and verify the predictions given in the Bible.

Fulfilled prophecy gives us the clearest evidence of the Bible's reliability. If we can't trust what it says about specific predicted events, how can we trust it for other important matters like our relationship to God and our eternal destiny?

Former atheist and Chicago news reporter Lee Strobel set out on a mission to use his investigative reporting skills to disprove the claims of the Bible. The problem was, this forced him to study the Bible for himself, which actually had the effect of leading to his unexpected conversion to Christianity. That's not all. He then authored a series of best-selling books[2] explaining various evidences for the Christian faith. When people take the time to research Scripture objectively, the results may take them by surprise.

The Bible is unique among all other books or religious documents, ancient or modern. No other book contains fulfilled prophecies like the Bible. If you will recall the chart from chapter 1, we learned that the Bible is made up of 66 books written by at least 40 authors over a period of about 1,500 years. These facts make fulfilled prophecy even more amazing. It's clear that indeed, "all Scripture is God-breathed" (2 Timothy 3:16) as God mysteriously spoke through prophets to deliver his message to the human race.

In a world where truth is considered to be relative and where the masses are encouraged or even strong-armed into accepting everyone's "truth" as valid, I often wonder if logic can still be used to persuade people. Personal feelings and ideologies often trump facts in the marketplace of ideas. Many people have become conditioned to accept the nonsensical in the name of pluralism and political correctness.

However, for the sincere truth-seeker, logic still serves its intended purpose. Facts are real and concrete. Truth is not relative, and our God-given ability to think logically is still one of the key things that separates us from the animals. Deep in our gut is a compass that points to true north despite the loud and deceptive voices of culture.

Contrary to what Bible critics say, we who believe that the Bible is true and accurate do not arrive at this conclusion by blind faith. Rather, it is a reasoned faith, an honest faith built on a large body of evidence. The Bible is not true because Christians say so. The Bible is true because it's based on fact. That being the case, then an honest observation of the evidence will bear this out. Fulfilled prophecy is a fact we can analyze and verify. Either it has occurred or it has not.

Faith is still required, of course. We can't "prove" the Bible is from God in a strict scientific sense that is repeatable and observable. We can't go back in time to show God speaking to Moses in a pillar of fire or the angel Gabriel delivering God's message to Daniel, but we can point to compelling patterns of evidence that overwhelmingly point to the Bible's divine authorship. This evidence comes in many forms (see chart), the most compelling of which is fulfilled prophecy.

APOLOGETICS/EVIDENCES FOR THE CHRISTIAN FAITH

historical/forensic evidence • manuscript evidence
archeology • scientific evidence • logical arguments
intelligent design • creation science
philosophical arguments • moral apologetics
internal evidence • external evidence • fulfilled prophecy

We highlighted the amazing fact of fulfilled prophecy briefly in chapter 1, and we'll expand on it here in greater detail. Before we look at some compelling examples of fulfilled prophecy, I'd like you to consider an analogy to help set the stage.

A Book That Tells the Future Accurately

Imagine that your parents received a mysterious gift at a baby shower a few weeks before you were born. In this book, specific details about your birth and future events in your life were predicted in vivid detail. The predictions did not cover every detail of your life, but it included all the major events. It predicted key childhood and adolescent milestones, the college you would attend, career milestones, the person you would marry, how many kids you would have (and even one of their names), how many grandchildren you would have, as well as all of your most trying setbacks and major accomplishments. It even predicted the time frame and details surrounding the end of your life. All told, there were hundreds of specific predictions about your life in this baby book.

At first, your parents assumed it was an odd attempt at a joke. They thought about discarding the strange gift, but decided to keep it out of sheer curiosity to see whether the first few predictions would even come close to being accurate. And they were! The details surrounding your birth were shockingly accurate and made even more sense after you were born. Peripheral details that your parents overlooked beforehand now came into full view and made the predictions that much more impressive.

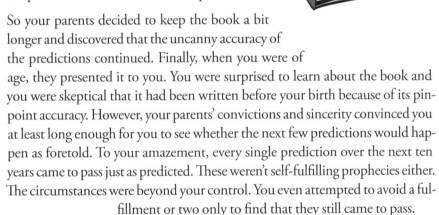

So your parents decided to keep the book a bit longer and discovered that the uncanny accuracy of the predictions continued. Finally, when you were of age, they presented it to you. You were surprised to learn about the book and you were skeptical that it had been written before your birth because of its pin-point accuracy. However, your parents' convictions and sincerity convinced you at least long enough for you to see whether the next few predictions would happen as foretold. To your amazement, every single prediction over the next ten years came to pass just as predicted. These weren't self-fulfilling prophecies either. The circumstances were beyond your control. You even attempted to avoid a fulfillment or two only to find that they still came to pass.

If that story were true, what would you conclude—that some deranged individual played a prank, made up this fairy tale, and just got lucky every single time? I suspect that as each prediction was fulfilled, your confidence in this book would grow until eventually you would come to trust this book implicitly. Its statistical track record would win you over as your confidence grew deeper with each passing fulfillment.

Such is the case with the Bible if we take the time to look at its prophecies. The Bible is not a book of fairy tales foisted upon us by a group of con artists. It is an intricately woven love letter given to a lost world. In an attempt to win our hearts and give our free will a chance to accept the truth, this love letter was crafted with a built-in proof of authenticity—fulfilled prophecy.

Prophecy experts cite that 28 percent of the Bible is prophecy, and 80 percent of those prophecies have already been fulfilled. Hundreds of specific predictions that are thousands of years old have been fulfilled to the exact detail. It would be somewhat impressive if only a few of them came to pass accurately, but the incredible fact is that Bible prophecy has a 100 percent fulfillment rate. The remaining 20 percent of yet unfulfilled prophecies are all future ones relating to end-time events. Now, I'd like you to keep this baby shower gift analogy in mind as we look at some specific examples of fulfilled Bible prophecy.

1/3RD PROPHECY

80% FULFILLED

20% STILL FUTURE

Specific Examples of Fulfilled Prophecies
Major World Empire Prophecies

In chapter 2 of the book of Daniel—written in the sixth century BC—the prophet Daniel, a Babylonian captive, interprets a dream for King Nebuchadnezzar, who had a vision of a statue. The statue had a head of gold, a chest and arms of silver, a belly and thighs of bronze, legs of iron, and feet and toes of iron mixed with clay. Impressive right? No, what's impressive is the interpretation of the dream.

In Daniel 2:39-42 as Daniel is speaking to King Nebuchadnezzar, we read,

After your kingdom comes to an end, another kingdom, inferior to yours, will rise to take your place. After that kingdom has fallen, yet a third kingdom, represented by bronze, will rise to rule the world. Following that kingdom, there will be a fourth one, as strong as iron. That kingdom will smash and crush all previous empires, just as iron smashes and crushes everything it strikes. The feet and toes you saw were a combination of iron and baked clay, showing that this kingdom will be divided. Like iron mixed with clay, it will have some of the strength of iron. But while some parts of it will be as strong as iron, other parts will be as weak as clay (NLT).

In verse 45, Daniel tells Nebuchadnezzar, "The great God was showing the king what will happen in the future. The dream is true, and its meaning is certain" (NLT).

History has proven Daniel's interpretation of Nebuchadnezzar's dream and his claim that it foretold the future in certain terms. From Daniel's time to our day, history records a succession of four increasingly larger empires symbolized by the metal that each was known for—Babylon, Medo-Persia, Greece, and Rome—and then a switch in which the fourth empire eventually breaks down into an unstable mix (iron and clay) of nation-states—with some strong and some weak. The final state of the empires will consist of ten toes that represent ten powerful rulers during the tribulation (more on that in a few chapters).

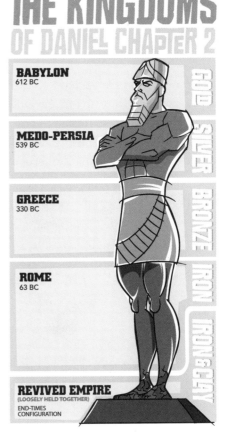

THE KINGDOMS OF DANIEL CHAPTER 2

BABYLON
612 BC

MEDO-PERSIA
539 BC

GREECE
330 BC

ROME
63 BC

REVIVED EMPIRE
(LOOSELY HELD TOGETHER)
END-TIMES CONFIGURATION

GOLD · SILVER · BRONZE · IRON · IRON & CLAY

So accurate were Daniel's predictions that critics have argued that the book of Daniel must have been written *after* those events took place, sometime during the second century BC. However, we know from modern textual studies that Daniel wrote in languages no longer used by the second century BC. Also, the book of Daniel had already long been part of the accepted Jewish canon, or what we now call the Old Testament. Fragments making up most of the book of Daniel were discovered in the Dead Sea Scrolls (150 BC–AD 60), demonstrating that the book of Daniel was already a well-established holy scripture for the Jewish people living in the ancient Qumran community during the second century BC.

Aside from those facts, we clearly see that the fourth empire did in fact split and break up into unstable nation-states. World War I, World War II, and even the current instability in Europe caused by the influx of millions of Middle Eastern refugees all bear witness to the "iron and clay" instability that is expected in the time of the end.

Any way you slice it, Daniel's prophecy has come true on every level, and critics don't know what to do with this passage. Every argument they have come up with has been dismantled by new manuscript evidence and our daily news.

How would Daniel have known that there would be four successive empires, each swallowing up the previous, followed next by a breakdown of the empire paradigm into an unstable confederation of countries? Because biblical prophecy is prerecorded history and compelling evidence that it was God himself who revealed this information through the prophets.

26 OF THE 109 MESSIANIC PROPHECIES

PROPHECY	PREDICTION	FULFILLMENT
Isaiah 7:14	born of a virgin	Luke 1:26-53
Micah 5:2	born in Bethlehem	Matthew 2:1
Hosea 11:1	flight into Egypt	Matthew 2:14
Jeremiah 31:15	to escape death	Matthew 2:16
Genesis 49:10	from the tribe of Judah	Luke 3:33
Isaiah 7:14	called Immanuel	Matthew 1:23
Isaiah 9:1-2	ministry in Galilee	Matthew 4:12-16
Zechariah 9:9	triumphal entry into Jerusalem	Matthew 21:1-11
Psalm 41:9	betrayed by a friend	Matthew 26:20-25
Zechariah 11:12	for 30 pieces of silver	Matthew 26:15
Zechariah 11:13	money used for potter's field	Matthew 26:6-7
Isaiah 53:3	rejected by Jews	John 1:11
Psalm 35:11	falsely accused	Matthew 26:59-68
Isaiah 53:7	silent before accusers	Matthew 27:12-14
Isaiah 50:6	hit and spit on	Mark 14:65
Isaiah 53:4-5	suffered for others (us)	Matthew 8:16-17
Isaiah 53:12	crucified with robbers	Matthew 27:38
Psalm 22:16	hands and feet pierced	John 20:25
Psalm 34:20	bones not broken	John 19:33
Psalm 22:18	lots cast for clothes	John 19:23-24
Psalm 22:15	thirsted on the cross	John 19:28
Psalm 69:21	and given vinegar	John 19:29
Psalm 22:1	"My God, why did you forsake me?"	Matthew 27:46
Isaiah 53:9	buried in tomb of rich	Matthew 27:57-61
Psalm 16:10	resurrection	Matthew 28:9
Psalm 68:18	ascension	Luke 24:50-51

Messianic Prophecies

If you'll recall the Christmas story, there was a godly old man named Simeon who was "eagerly waiting for the Messiah to come" (Luke 2:25 NLT). There were also Magi, or wise men from the East, who arrived sometime after Jesus's birth (Matthew 2:1). And of course, just before the kickoff of Jesus's earthly ministry, John the Baptist understood that his calling was to prepare the way for the Messiah. Luke 3:15 even goes so far as to say, "Everyone was expecting the Messiah to come soon."

This begs the question: How did people know? Why were so many expecting the Messiah? It was because of the many prophecies foretelling the time frame and conditions for his arrival.

There are 109 separate and distinct prophecies, or more than 300 if you include prophecies that are repeated in some form, about the Messiah that were fulfilled at Jesus's first coming. Specific details regarding the timing, conditions, lineage, and city of his birth; the nature of his life and ministry; and the specifics of his death, burial, and resurrection were all foretold long ago in the Old Testament. Daniel chapter 9 even provided the exact time frame for his first coming!

Studies have been done calculating the probability of these prophecies being fulfilled by one person. Even if only four of these prophecies were fulfilled by one person, the probability of that happening would be 1 in 10 trillion. The odds of 48 prophecies being fulfilled by one person is one in a trillion trillion trillion trillion trillion trillion trillion trillion trillion trillion trillion trillion trillion![3]

Read the following two verses and ask yourself who this passage is talking about:

> He was pierced for our transgressions,
>   he was crushed for our iniquities;
> the punishment that brought us peace was on him,
>   and by his wounds we are healed.
> We all, like sheep, have gone astray, each of us has turned to our
> own way; and the LORD has laid on him the iniquity of us all
> (Isaiah 53:5-6).

That was written eight centuries before Jesus came, yet it may as well have been from John chapter 3.

In Luke chapter 24, after the resurrection, Jesus provided an Old Testament survey to a couple of his disciples, in which he demonstrated how he fulfilled the Old Testament prophecies about the Messiah. In verse 27, we read, "Beginning with Moses and all the Prophets, he explained to them what was said in all the Scriptures concerning himself." Indeed, Jesus is all over the Old Testament and fulfilled a staggering number of prophecies at his first coming.

MORE EXAMPLES OF FULFILLED PROPHECY

300+ prophecies of 1st coming • destruction of the city of Tyre
destruction of the city of Sidon • Persian king Cyrus foretold
fall of Babylonian Empire • rise of Medo-Persian Empire
rise of Greek Empire • rise of Roman Empire • disintegration
of Roman Empire • 1st and 2nd dispersions of Israel
1st and 2nd regathering • worldwide persecution of the Jewish people
preservation of the Jewish people • rebirth of Israel
unification of Israel at rebirth • economic stability of Israel
strong military of Israel • Israel to be attacked by neighbors
reoccupation of Jerusalem • reclamation of Israel's unusable land
Jewish desire to rebuild the temple in Jerusalem • Israel to be center of
world conflict after rebirth • Russia and Iran would form an alliance

The Jewish People

The Jewish people are a living testimony to God's sovereignty over fulfilled prophecy. The Scriptures and the Savior came through the Jewish people, and they play a key role in end-times prophecy. That is the reason there has been a millennia-long satanic hatred of the Jews that shows up throughout the pages of Scripture and world history. As God's chosen people, the Jews have a remarkable and miraculous history, all foretold in Bible prophecy.

In all of history there has never been another people group who has lost their land, been scattered all over the world, persecuted almost everywhere they have gone, maintained their cultural identity, and returned to their original homeland after nearly 2,000 years.

There are many Old and New Testament prophecies concerning the Jewish people. From the Abrahamic covenant to events of our day, we see the very clear fulfillment of prophecies exactly as they were foretold by the prophets, the apostles, and by Jesus himself.

For example, the Bible predicted there would be two dispersions and two occasions where the Jewish people would be regathered to their land (Isaiah 11:11). The first occurred in 605 BC, when Judah was conquered and the Jewish survivors were taken captive to Babylon and returned 70 years later to their land, just as predicted. The second dispersion occurred in AD 70, when the Romans destroyed Jerusalem, thus scattering the Jewish people all over the known world.

Following that, the Jewish people experienced major ongoing persecution that pushed many of them to even farther reaches of the world—most notably the 1492 Edict of Expulsion in Spain, the pogroms in Russia, and the Holocaust during WWII at the hands of Hitler's Nazi Germany.

QUICK FACT: DID YOU KNOW...

that new research shows Columbus was very likely a secret Jew who hid his identity *(known as Marranos)* during the oppressive Spanish inquisitions and that his real purpose for the voyage was to find a safe haven for the Jewish people?

In the late 1800s and early 1900s Jews began returning to their land the second time due to such hardships and persecution. They did not officially have a national homeland until, miraculously, after WWII, the nation of Israel was literally reborn "in a day" (Isaiah 66:8) on May 14, 1948. There are also many prophecies in the Bible requiring Jewish control of Jerusalem (see Zechariah 8:4-8; 12:1-3; Daniel 9:27; Matthew 24:15-18; 2 Thessalonians 2:3-4), which were fulfilled in 1967 as a result of the Six-Day War.

Supernatural Fingerprints

Bible prophecy was one of the most compelling evidences that caused me to consider the claims of Christianity prior to my becoming a Christian. Fulfilled prophecy and my growing awareness of the intricate cohesion of Scripture made me reevaluate my position that the Bible was just a prescientific-age book of religious fairy tales. The more I studied its pages, the more I found an internal cracking of my doubts and a shift in my convictions. There were just too many small details that were subtly pointing to a sovereign Author.

I believe God uses prophecy to open people's eyes to the fact that only a divine being who is master over time could have inspired these prophecies. Fulfilled prophecy demonstrates that the Bible is of divine origin and can, therefore, be trusted in matters of faith such as salvation and eternity.

If you happen to be reading this book and have not yet seriously considered the claims of the Bible, I challenge you (in a friendly way, not in a duel-to-the-death kind of way) to check out some of these prophecies for yourself and see if there is any other explanation except that they are inspired by God.

CHAPTER 3

What Are the Practical Benefits of Studying Bible Prophecy?

Blessed is the one who reads aloud the words of this prophecy, and blessed are those who hear it and take to heart what is written in it, because the time is near.

REVELATION 1:3

With the pressures of life and the very real struggles people face, some believers may wonder if studying Bible prophecy is relevant to their daily lives. Wouldn't it be more practical to spend time studying scripture that relates to topics such as work, marriage, raising kids, resisting temptation, or living without worry? All of those are extremely valid areas of study, but I have also found that studying Bible prophecy has some overarching practical benefits that are critically important to our daily lives as believers in Jesus Christ.

Over the years as I have studied Bible prophecy, I've noticed that it affects the way I live. As I am reminded that Christ's return is drawing closer and that many people I know still need to turn to Christ for salvation, there are three things that happen internally.

Three Key Benefits

The first is I find myself wanting to grow spiritually and live with more purity and dedication in a world that seems to be growing darker by the day. I find that I have more passion and resolve to live the way Christ calls us to live as I see the Bible come to life and as I anticipate his return.

Second, I find myself wanting to point others to Jesus because I want as many people as possible with me in heaven when the dust settles.

Third, I find myself living with a much clearer perspective as I view world events through the eyes of Bible prophecy. Armed with a deeper trust and knowledge that God has a specific plan and that he keeps his promises, I'm more able to live courageously and purposefully in the face of an increasingly unstable world.

Ultimately, I've found that the study of prophecy helps me to grow in my faith, share my faith, and see with the eyes of faith.

DISCIPLESHIP
To grow spiritually.

EVANGELISM
Telling others about Jesus's gift of salvation.

BIBLICAL WORLDVIEW
Understanding the world in light of biblical truth.

Growing Spiritually Mature

There's an unholy trinity we have to face down. We fight the world, the flesh, and the devil on a daily basis. Sounds like an old-school sermon, but it's as true as it ever was. First, you and I live in a fallen world system that constantly tries to draw us away from a life of faith and obedience. With ever increasing pull, the world is darkening and tempting us to lower our standards.

Second, there's a battle within us. You and I live in a fallen body that has a sin nature. We have a natural bent toward sinfully destructive thoughts, actions, and patterns. We can cater to our flesh or our Spirit. When we accepted Christ, we received the Holy Spirit, who gives us power to overcome sin. Our flesh and our spirit war against each other. We have to decide daily which one we'll feed, and which one we'll starve.

> Romans 7:19-20 — For I do not do the good I want to do, but the evil I do not want to do—this I keep on doing. Now if I do what I do not want to do, it is no longer I who do it, but it is sin living in me that does it.

Third, you and I have a fallen enemy. His name is Satan. He doesn't have red horns and a pitchfork. He morphs. He lies. He comes as an "angel of light" (2 Corinthians 11:14). He's real and he wants to destroy you. Not hurt. Not damage. *Destroy.* John 10:10 states that Jesus came to give "life to the fullest," but we often overlook the first part of the verse. It informs us that the enemy comes to "steal and kill and destroy."

QUICK FACT: DID YOU KNOW...

A 2009 study showed that 4 out of 10 self-described Christians strongly agreed that Satan "is not a living being but is a symbol of evil" and that only 2.5 out of 10 believe he is a real being?

Source: https://www.barna.com/research/most-american-christians-do-not-believe-that-satan-or-the-holy-spirit-exist/

Your eternal enemy wants to keep you from salvation. If he can't do that, he wants to minimize your effectiveness and hurt you so that he can hurt God, who loves you. The worst way to hurt a parent is to hurt their child. The Bible tells us that when Satan rebelled against God, he convinced one-third of the angels in heaven to rebel with him. They are now fallen angels who do his bidding in the unseen realm all around the globe. So there is a very real unseen battle going on around us that leverages the fallen world and our sin nature to do everything possible to steal, kill, and destroy. A study of Bible prophecy brings this battle and its future results into clear view. We know how it is going to end.

What we're really talking about is discipleship. Very simply, discipleship is following and obeying Jesus, which leads to spiritual growth. It means we are learning to be like Jesus or growing toward Christlikeness. We will never be sinless or perfect, but should see growth in our lives as we overcome sin and serve Jesus through our actions and decisions. Assuming you are a Christian, you have probably faced some struggles and want to grow in your faith and grow closer in your walk with the Lord. You want to serve Jesus through a life of passionate commitment and wholehearted devotion. You want to be strong in the face of temptation. And, by the way, if you are not yet a Christian, please keep reading! There is a very important chapter for you later in the book.

I've found that a personal study of prophecy drives people into Scripture so that they learn how to get answers for themselves. More importantly, the more we get into Scripture, the more Scripture gets into us. This is always a good thing.

The Bible is a supernatural book and it does supernatural things to us as we digest it. Hebrews 4:12 says, "The word of God is alive and active. Sharper than any double-edged sword, it penetrates even to dividing soul and spirit, joints and marrow; it judges the thoughts and attitudes of the heart." As you study Bible prophecy, you have no choice but to grow as a disciple.

QUICK FACT: DID YOU KNOW...

that a study of Bible prophecy intersects with every key category of Christian theology?

Theology Proper:	The Nature and Attributes of God
God the Father:	The First Person of the Trinity
Christology:	The Second Person of the Trinity
Pneumatology:	The Third Person of the Trinity
Cosmology:	The Study of Things Created
Anthropology:	The Study of Humanity
Angelology:	The Study of Angels
Theodicy:	The Study of Allowance of Evil
Hamartiology:	The Study of Sin
Soteriology:	The Study of Salvation
Ecclesiology:	The Study of Church
Eschatology:	The Study of Last Things

Desiring to Share Christ

The New Testament informs us that the church, which includes every true believer, will be raptured (suddenly taken to be with Christ) prior to a terrible time of judgment that is coming upon the whole world. I'll explain this more clearly in chapter 4 and cover the different views of the rapture in chapter 6, but I am overwhelmingly convinced the rapture takes place prior to the tribulation period. This should be a major motivating factor for sharing our faith. If people can escape the coming judgment by accepting Christ's offer of forgiveness, don't we want our friends and loved ones to know about it?

God always warns before he judges. He did it for the wicked city of Nineveh. He did it for Sodom and Gomorrah. And he did it for the world prior to the flood of Noah's day. In 2 Peter 3:9 we read, "The Lord is not slow in keeping his promise, as some understand slowness. Instead he is patient with you, not wanting anyone to perish, but everyone to come to repentance." From Genesis to Revelation, Scripture is clear that God has done everything to save us from his necessary judgment of sin. He demonstrated this by sending his perfect, sinless Son to die in our place. The gift of salvation is already available for the taking if we will accept it. But God is a gentleman. He won't force us to accept his gift. He lets us choose our own destiny.

What's all this talk of judgment and wrath? Isn't he a God of love? Yes, he is, but perfect love requires judgment. If someone were to torture and murder you, it would not be loving toward you if God let that horrific sin go unpunished. God is holy and must punish sin. Like oil and water, holiness and sin do not mix. If we see a sign outside an electrical substation that reads "Danger. Keep Out!" we don't scoff at the sign and say it is just a scare tactic. We understand that the purpose of the sign is up to keep us from pain and loss. Human flesh and high-voltage electricity don't play nice together.

I've heard it said, "God doesn't send people to hell. He rescues people *from* hell." Judgment is the default response to sin. It's just a fact; it is a fixed spiritual law that undergirds reality—similar to the fixed laws of physics that govern our physical world. A holy God can't overlook sin, but this same holy God did everything possible to save you and me from judgment. He sent his own Son to pay for our sins on the cross, and he gave us a clear and detailed love letter verified by hundreds of fulfilled prophecies. In addition to that, he's given us 2,000 years since the time of his resurrection so that the message could spread to every corner of the world.

All of the verses in the Bible about God's wrath and judgment are his "Danger. Keep Out!" signs. Second Peter 3:9 says point blank that God is "not wanting

anyone to perish, but everyone to come to repentance," but he can't force us to turn to him. You and I have an important message to share, and we have a short time to share it. We have the cure to the problems of this world, and it's time for us to share it boldly. Whether by our own death or by Christ's return, our time is limited. We need to post "Danger. Keep Out!" signs by how we live and what we talk about. Bible prophecy and the nearness of Christ's return will motivate us to tell others about God's incredible gift of salvation.

Viewing Life with an Eternal Perspective

Just as *fulfilled* prophecy offers support to the thought that God wrote the Bible, a study of *future* prophecy helps us see life through a new lens. A lens that suddenly makes the amazing future prophetic events just as real and miraculous as Moses parting the Red Sea, Elijah calling fire down from the sky, or Jesus raising Lazarus from the dead. The last days are full of many supernatural events that have yet to unfold. As we study Bible history, we will better understand Bible prophecy. The truth about the past is connected to the truth about the future. It's no wonder that reliability of Scripture has come under unrelenting attack during the same time that the theory of evolution has come to permeate culture the past 150-plus years. If the enemy can blur the truth of the past, he can blur the truth of the future. Understanding biblical truth about the past and future gives us a solid biblical worldview—a proper perspective about God's activity and his soon return.

Here's how that works on a practical level—and I share this from personal experience. Life pressures, petty distractions, and the temptations of the world carry less weight when you have this perspective. Serving others through everyday opportunities, volunteering at church, or through mission trips take on new meaning. Loving and serving your spouse and honoring your relationship commitments take on a greater eternal value. Facing the daily news and the insanity, lawlessness, and instability in the world no longer shakes you. It's like having a secret pair of glasses that turns the chaos into order. Maintaining a sense of purpose and calling happens as a result of this perspective. Seeing God at work in your life and the world at large is an added blessing. Gaining an increasing love and respect for God's Word is a result of this perspective. Living by well-reasoned faith, not by sight, is a result as well.

Practical Christianity

If you and I take on the important task of studying prophecy and end-time events, we will continue to grow deeper in our faith, reach more people for Christ, and experience a more abundant and fearless life. Those three components combine to give us a faith that is more relevant than we've ever had before. We also become watchmen and women on the wall. That's Christianese for being able to warn others of the coming judgment and taking full advantage of the current wide-open door to invite people to rush into the arms of a loving Savior who died for them. As I mentioned in chapter 1, everyone is wondering what in the world is going on, and the Bible has the answers.

The bottom line is that Bible prophecy is extremely practical, and God clearly wants us to study it, as demonstrated by Revelation 1:3, which was cited at the beginning of this chapter. Don't let the enemy's attempts to confuse the issues blind you to the amazing practical blessings that are yours when you study Bible prophecy.

Okay, now it's about to get fun. It's time to get into the meat of this book as we define some of the key terms you need to know so you can understand end-times prophecy. Let's dig in!

PART 2:

THE KEY BUILDING BLOCKS OF BIBLE PROPHECY

CHAPTER 4

Key Terms Defined

All Scripture is God-breathed and is useful for teaching, rebuking, correcting, and training in righteousness.

2 TIMOTHY 3:16

I remember the first weekend my stepbrother came home from completing basic training in the Army. He was the same stepbrother I'd had before, except now he had a short haircut and talked in a strange new language. Half of his sentences included acronyms in them. He spoke about doing PT and passing his APFT and how his BDUs had to be maintained. He mentioned people who were XOs and how he and his unit would go out in the field to learn TACSOPs. After 16 weeks of eating and sleeping Army, the acronyms were so ingrained into his everyday language that he didn't even realize civilians like me had no clue as to what he was talking about.

Christians can do this as well. We can unknowingly talk in code language. In this book, I have attempted to stay away from using Christianese—you know, those five-dollar theological words or phrases that make you feel like Alex Trebek is about to correct your pronunciation of an obscure French military term. "Thank you, Alex. I'll take *MAKE ME FEEL STUPID* for a thousand dollars, please."

ADVANCED ROCKET SCIENCE	YOU'LL NEED A DOCTORATE FOR THIS ONE	MAKE ME FEEL STUPID	MANDARIN LINGUISTICS	PHRASES YOU'VE NEVER HEARD BEFORE	FILL-IN-THE-BLANK PERIODIC TABLE
$200					$200
$400			$400		$400
$600	$600		$600		$600
$800	$800		$800	$800	$800
$1000	$1000	$1000	$1000	$1000	$1000

I don't want this book to make you feel that way. It is designed to serve as a funnel that gathers a lot of seemingly vague information and pulls it together to move you from confusion and ambiguity to a clear understanding of the key components of Bible prophecy. You may already know a bit about the following key terms, but my assumption is that most readers will find the following list helpful for getting up to speed quickly. This list is not exhaustive by any means, but it clarifies the key terms that have shown up in pop culture but usually in an inaccurate way. Correctly understanding these basic terms will help provide you with a firm footing for the chapters that follow. I have framed each key term in the form of a question.

The Key Terms
What is the church?

The *church* is not a building, denomination, or religious system. The church consists of all true believers who have accepted God's offer of forgiveness and asked Jesus to be their personal Savior. The church consists of people, not buildings. Buildings merely serve as places for the church to gather. When Scripture talks about the church, it is speaking of either a local group of believers, or the universal invisible church that consists of all true believers worldwide.

The word *church* comes from the New Testament Greek word *ekklesia,* which means "a gathering" or "an assembly." The local church is designed to live in community and is relational and supportive in nature. The universal church, made up of all believers everywhere, is also known as "the body of Christ" (1 Corinthians 12:27).

What is the church age?

The *church age* is the time period we are currently living in. It is also known as the *age of grace* because anyone can turn to Jesus and receive the grace and forgiveness he offers. Once a person turns away from his or her sins and receives Christ as Savior, he or she becomes part of the church.

The church age began on the *Day of Pentecost,* fifty days after Jesus's resurrection (and ten days after his ascension), at which time he sent the Holy Spirit to indwell his followers, as promised in Acts 1:3-8. The church age will end at the time of the rapture, when the church is removed from the world.

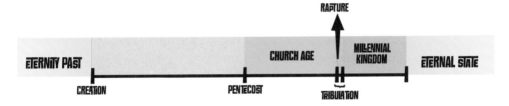

What is the rapture?

The rapture is when the universal church will instantaneously be taken up to heaven. This will include all believers who are alive on the earth at the time, and the resurrection of all church-age believers from the grave. The term *rapture* refers to a catching away, a sudden taking up of all true believers to be with the Lord. There are three main views regarding the timing of this future event—we will cover those in chapter 6.

The term *rapture* comes from *rapturo*, which is from the Latin translation of the New Testament Greek word *harpazo. Harpazo* is found in the key biblical text concerning the rapture,

1 Thessalonians 4:13-18. First Corinthians 15:51-52 is another passage that sheds light on this mysterious event.

What is the tribulation?

The *tribulation* is a future seven-year period when God's wrath finally comes to judge evil in the world after a long period of grace known as the church age. The *tribulation period* is distinct from the trials and tribulations that we all face as we live in a fallen world. This distinct future period will be a time of tremendous upheaval, unrestrained evil, unprecedented physical cataclysms, and extreme supernatural phenomena.

The tribulation period is also known as "the time of Jacob's [Israel's] trouble" (Jeremiah 30:7 nkjv), "the Day of the Lord" (Isaiah 2:12; Joel 1:15; 1 Thessalonians 5:2 nkjv), "a time of distress" (Daniel 12:1; see also Zephaniah 1:15), and the seventieth week of Daniel (Daniel 9). The second half (3.5 years) of the tribulation period is also known as *the great tribulation* (Matthew 24:21 nkjv) because of the increased intensity of the outpouring of God's wrath. Most of the book of Revelation concerns this future period of time. God's purpose for the tribulation period is to judge evil, utterly defeat Satan, and complete his plan of salvation for the people of Israel.

Bible teachers differ on their understanding of whether or not the church will go through some or all of the tribulation. I will cover those views in chapter 6 and let you decide for yourself. It is my strong belief that the church will be raptured prior to the beginning of the tribulation period. There are many reasons for this, which I will unpack in chapter 6.

What is the millennium?

The *millennium* is a future 1,000-year period that begins after Christ's return to Earth at the end of the tribulation. During this time, Satan will be bound in what is known as the abyss or pit, and Christ will establish his perfect kingdom on Earth, ruling from Jerusalem. The resurrected and raptured church will assist Jesus in ruling the world.

The purposes of this period are (1) to fulfill God's Old Testament promises for the future kingdom of Israel, which will have a ruler from the line of David, and (2) to demonstrate that even in a perfect world with a perfect ruler, mankind will still choose to rebel against God. This will be clearly demonstrated when Satan is let loose at the end of the millennium for one last battle. He will then attempt to convince the people of the world to join him in one last rebellion against God. Many will choose to join sides with him. After this final battle, Satan will be defeated and cast into the Lake of Fire, where he will remain forever.

Bible teachers differ on whether the millennium is figurative or literal. I will cover the different views of the millennium in chapter 7. It is my firm belief that the millennium is a future, literal 1,000-year period that begins after Christ's return at the end of the tribulation. It is a future period during which Satan will be bound and Christ will rule the world perfectly from Jerusalem.

What is the eternal state?

The eternal state is the final condition of the universe after all is said and done. After the rapture, tribulation, and millennial kingdom, Scripture tells us the old heaven and earth will be dissolved and a new heaven and earth will be created in absolute perfection and will last for eternity. Revelation 21–22 provides us with an amazing description of this final state. There will be no sorrow, no sin, no suffering, no pain, no death, and no evil. We will enjoy unending and perfect unity with Christ and experience the fullness of his blessings.

Revelation 21 describes the heavenly Jerusalem coming down from God. This heavenly Jerusalem might already exist now. Jesus may have been talking about the New Jerusalem when he told his disciples he was going away to make a dwelling place or mansion for each of his followers (John 14:2).

Who is the antichrist?

The *antichrist* is a future world ruler who will rise to power during the tribulation period. His identity will be clearly revealed when he confirms a covenant or treaty between Israel and some other countries. *Anti* means "against," and it also means "instead of." This man will be looked at as a type of savior of the world, someone whom people will flock to during a time of unprecedented turmoil. He will be against Christ and will demand to be worshipped in the place of Christ, the true God.

The antichrist will rise as a man of peace but will quickly turn violent. He will be the most vicious and most powerful dictator the world has ever seen. He is mentioned many times in the Old and New Testaments and is given many different names that describe his nature.

WHO IS THE ANTICHRIST?

"the little horn"	**Daniel 7:8**
"a fierce-looking king"	**Daniel 8:23**
"a master of intrigue"	**Daniel 8:23**
"the ruler who will come"	**Daniel 9:26**
"a contemptible person"	**Daniel 11:21**
"a shepherd who will not care"	**Zechariah 11:16**
"a worthless shepherd"	**Zechariah 11:16-17**
"man of lawlessness"	**2 Thessalonians 2:3**
"the lawless one"	**2 Thessalonians 2:8-9**
"the rider on the white horse"	**Revelation 6:2**
"a beast"	**Revelation 13:1**

Who is the false prophet?

The *false prophet* is a world religious leader who will unite the people of the earth and cause them to worship the antichrist. He is described in Revelation 13:11-15. He will be permitted, by God, to display supernatural signs and wonders. In the same way that the antichrist will be the worst dictator of all time, the false prophet will be the worst false religious leader of all time.

Satan, the antichrist, and the false prophet will make up what is essentially a counterfeit unholy trinity. Instead of the true holy Trinity, which is made up of the Father, Son, and Holy Spirit, the world will be ruled by this false unholy trinity.

At the end of the tribulation period, when Christ returns to Earth, both the beast and the false prophet will be thrown alive into the Lake of Fire.

What is the apocalypse?

In today's pop culture, the term *apocalypse* has generally come to refer to destruction, the end of the world, or terrible judgment. But those meanings aren't biblically accurate. In Scripture, the word *apocalypse* actually means "the revealing" or "the unveiling." It comes from the New Testament Greek word *apokalupsis*. The association with the book of Revelation comes from Revelation 1:1. In that passage, the first two words could be read "the uncovering" or "the unveiling" instead of "the revelation." Here, Jesus said he will uncover the future for the apostle John to write down. While Revelation does describe the judgment that will take place during the tribulation period, it also begins with three chapters of instruction to the churches and ends with a description of the future beauty and perfection of the millennial kingdom, the New Jerusalem, and the new heavens and earth.

What is Armageddon?

Similar to the term *apocalypse*, *Armageddon* has come to refer to destruction and judgment. You may also hear people talk about the Battle of Armageddon.

For clarity's sake, the term *Armageddon* basically refers to the mountains or hills of Megiddo. *Har* means "mountain" in Hebrew and refers to the literal physical place where the armies will gather to attempt to fight Christ at the end of the tribulation period, according to Revelation 16:16. This place is in Megiddo, a vast plain south of present-day Haifa, Israel. It is the plain where many biblical and other historic battles have been fought over the centuries. It is a perfect staging area for armies. In fact, Alexander the Great was said to have stated there was not a better battlefield on the whole earth.

When the Bible speaks of the Battle of Armageddon, it is referring to a huge war that will culminate in Christ's return, at which time he will defeat the antichrist and his armies.

The Next Step

Now that we have defined the key terms that will help us better understand the most prominent aspects of Bible prophecy, let's continue building on this framework. Next, we will look at the four interpretation methods used to understand Bible prophecy.

CHAPTER 5

The Four Interpretation Methods

For God is not the author of confusion but of peace, as in all the churches of the saints.

1 CORINTHIANS 14:33 (NKJV)

As we discuss interpretation methods in this chapter and the various views of the timing and nature of the rapture and the millennium in the next two chapters, I believe it is appropriate to talk about Christian unity. Far too often I've seen Christians shoot each other down because of differing views about secondary issues on which there is room for legitimate disagreement.

These friendly-fire Christians waste precious time and energy on things that aren't of greatest importance. Good people can disagree. It's naïve to assume that all Christians will agree on every single point. We all have different backgrounds and journeys, and we are all at different points in our discipleship or spiritual growth.

Yes, doctrine is important. Yes, ideas have consequences. But, unless it's a deal breaker, we need to stand shoulder to shoulder with our fellow believers as we attempt to reach a lost world for Christ.

Unity and Humility

To cite a seventeenth-century theologian, "In essentials unity, in nonessentials liberty, in all things charity."[4] There are beliefs that are essential or fundamental to true Christianity, and there are also secondary nonessential issues that allow room for debate.

FUNDAMENTAL BELIEFS FOR CHRISTIANS INCLUDE:

1. Jesus is God the Son, the second member of the Trinity
2. He was born of a virgin
3. His sacrificial blood alone can save you from the penalty of sin
4. He was raised from the dead
5. He is coming back

QUICK QUESTION:
HOW DOES ONE BECOME A CHRISTIAN?
Pause here and go to chapter 20 to find out!

The views we have regarding the end times fall into this second category. I wrestle with calling them nonessentials because every word in Scripture is important and inspired by God. And I believe a proper understanding of Bible prophecy has major implications that guide our thinking and behavior. But the secondary issues are labeled as such in the sense that they do not determine whether or not someone is saved. It is possible for true believers to disagree on certain issues. We're all growing and learning as we study God's Word and seek to follow God's ways.

In addition to approaching the subject of prophetic interpretation with unity, I also believe we should approach it with extreme humility. Those who believe they have every single prophetic detail figured out are deceiving themselves.

There are very smart, godly, dedicated Christians who hold different views of the end times.

Prophecy is a complex subject, and admittedly it takes quite a bit of study to understand and develop clear convictions. Also, Scripture doesn't give us all the details or an exact timeline for every end-time event. As we look forward to prophetic events it's like watching a show on a nine-inch black-and-white TV. There's enough information to follow the story, but there are many details we can't quite make out. We learn from 1 Corinthians 13:12 that "now we see only a reflection as in a mirror; then we shall see face to face."

Why All the Mystery?

God is intentionally mysterious. Daniel 2:22 tells us as much. There we read, "He reveals deep and hidden things; he knows what lies in darkness, and light dwells with him." Later in verse 47 of the same chapter, God is described as being "a revealer of mysteries."

There are at least two key reasons for God's mysterious treatment of end-time events.

First, we need to remember that we are in a spiritual war that has been raging for ages. The enemy, Satan, is real, and he knows the Bible well.

Through his millennia-long rebellion against the Creator, Satan has patiently and repeatedly attempted to undermine God's plan of redemption. Scripture tells us Satan will fail and be judged eternally in the Lake of Fire. Even so, his pride and self-deceit convince him that there remains a way to usurp God's rightful and immovable place on heaven's throne.

> Genesis 3:15—I will put enmity between you and the woman, and between your offspring and hers; he will crush your head, and you will strike his heel.

In Genesis 3:15 we have the Bible's first messianic prophecy, which tells us that the seed (or offspring) of the woman will one day crush the head of the serpent (Satan). Ever since then, Satan has been trying to throw God's plan off track by any means possible, including attempts to corrupt all flesh (Genesis 6), destroy the Jews through whom the seed of the woman would come (multiple times throughout history), kill Jesus before he was two years old, tempt Jesus in the desert at the beginning of his ministry, and kill Jesus on a Roman cross.

The last attempt mentioned above appeared to succeed, but was sovereignly planned by God and was followed by the resurrection of Christ—history's most powerful counterpunch. Satan should have seen it coming, but he missed it. For all intents and purposes, his head was now crushed. Jesus beat sin on the cross, and he beat death at the resurrection. That Jesus would bring victory through his death was prophesied in the ancient writings, but veiled just enough to confuse the enemy. The Lord has employed similar tactical strategies with regard to end-time prophecies. He is omniscient and has surely written prophecy in such a way that it will encourage and equip believers, while at the same time, confuse and thwart the enemy. A good general never makes his intelligence report available to his enemy. He gives needed information to his troops and veiled information to the enemy.

Second, I believe God is intentionally mysterious because that forces us to read his Word more carefully, and it is there that he can change us. He leads us on a lifelong journey of discovery and pursuit of himself, a God whose depth of blessing has no end. The knowledge of God and the mind of Christ are endless gold mines. The mystery of God encourages us to pursue him as we journey through life.

With regard to mysteries about the last days, ultimately, what we're after is truth and Christian unity, not winning debates. Approach Scripture with that attitude and with much prayer, and the Holy Spirit will honor your sincere truth-seeking and pure motives with clarity and conviction about end-time events.

The Views

With all that in mind, the fact remains that there are different methods of interpretation that will impact how you and I understand end-time events. Rather than allowing this to be a deterrent to studying Bible prophecy, we should let it serve as a motivator for each of us to study these things for ourselves. The interpretation method you choose will greatly affect your view about Christ's return.

The four interpretation methods described over the next few pages should be evaluated carefully, prayerfully, and honestly. I hold to the futurist position for the reasons I cite later, but I want to acknowledge again that smart and godly Christian teachers hold different views on how to interpret Bible prophecy and particularly the book of Revelation. Within this in-house debate, there are four main ways people have viewed Revelation over the centuries: *idealist, preterist, historicist,* and *futurist.*

The Idealist View: Prophecy Is All Symbolic

This view is also sometimes referred to as the *spiritual view.* This is because it allegorizes or spiritualizes prophetic texts, including those in the book of Revelation. This school of thought arose around AD 190 from the region of Alexandria, Egypt, and was adopted by the fifth-century theologian Augustine of Hippo. Augustine applied this spiritualization-only approach to prophetic texts, unlike the Alexandrians, who applied it to most or all of Scripture. Augustine's teaching became the dominant view of the Roman Catholic Church and carried over into the Protestant Reformation, which was spurred largely by Martin Luther and John Calvin.

ST. AUGUSTINE

The main problem with allegorizing certain prophetic sections of Scripture is that we open ourselves to the risk of making a passage say something it doesn't intend to say. The interpreter becomes the standard instead of Scripture itself. This has led people to come up with wildly varying meanings of prophetic texts, and leaves us with little confidence that certain passages can truly be understood.

Also, if we can allegorize one portion of Scripture, what's to say we can't allegorize other portions or even the entire Bible? Where does it stop? If everything has the potential for allegory, the entirety of Scripture loses its authority and ultimately any clear, straightforward meaning.

Another discrediting factor of this view is that the clear prophecies of the first coming of Christ were fulfilled literally. Why, then, would we switch the interpretive rules and view future prophecies as allegory? Doing that forces us to take two inconsistent approaches to interpreting Bible prophecy. It makes more sense to interpret future prophecies as being fulfilled literally, just as past prophecies were.

The Preterist View: The Prophecies Already Happened

The basic claim of this view is that Bible prophecy is already Bible history. The preterist view says that the book of Revelation refers to first-century events rather than future ones.

Within this view there are two lines of thought. Some teachers assert that part of the book of Revelation has already occurred (partial preterism), while others teach that all of it took place in the past (full preterism)—namely, in AD 70, when the Romans destroyed Jerusalem.

This view arose in the mid-1500s in an attempt to help the Roman Catholic Church counter the arguments of Protestants during the Reformation. The reformers held the historicist view (described next) and interpreted the antichrist, the apostate church, and other negative elements in the book of Revelation as being representative of the Roman Catholic Church and the Pope. They successfully painted sixteenth-century Roman Catholicism as an apostate entity that persecuted true believers.

Catholic theologians developed the preterist view in an attempt to sway popular belief away from these negative connotations by teaching that the events of Revelation had already occurred in the first century. This is still the primary view of Roman Catholics, and it has since carried over into some Protestant denominations.

There are major problems with this view as well. The main one is that John wrote the book of Revelation around AD 95 while exiled on the Island of Patmos, about 15 years *after* the fall of Jerusalem.

This is problematic mainly from a chronological perspective. Why would John write such a detailed book specifically about prophecy—which is by nature future—then choose to write about events that had taken place 15 years prior to the writing of the book?

Yet another problem with this view is that it does not account for several marquee events in the book of Revelation that have no historical equivalent. Preterists claim these events have already happened, but they cannot point to clear evidence those events were fulfilled in the past.

For example, the book of Revelation details a physical return of Christ to the earth witnessed by all who are alive at that time, a complete and decisive defeat of Satan at Christ's return, a great white throne judgment of every unbeliever, and other significant events which clearly have not occurred yet.

Similar to the idealist view, the preterist view necessarily allegorizes various details of Bible prophecy, which leaves us running into the same problem that idealists do. We're left with no clear way of knowing which passages are allegorical, and which aren't.

The Historicist View: Prophecy Is an Overview of History

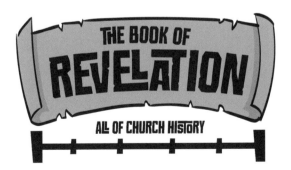

This view first appeared around AD 300 and attempts to interpret Revelation simply as a symbolic representation of history—of all that has taken place and will take place in church history from John's time to the end. This view was popular during the Reformation era but has many problems, and there are numerous versions of it.

This view also allegorizes Scripture, and each generation of its adopters has changed the meaning of allegorized symbols based on events, rulers, and conditions of their day. In other words, the way Bible prophecy is interpreted constantly changes, leaving us uncertain as to what the Bible really is saying. This is the weakest of the four views and is not very popular today.

The Futurist View: Prophecy Is Literally Going to Happen as Stated

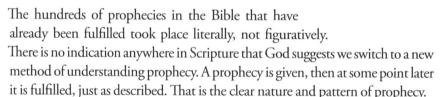

This view teaches that the prophetic events described in Revelation are yet future. It holds that these events and related ones described in the Old Testament will occur literally in the future and are to be understood by the plain sense of the text. The book of Revelation clearly claims to be prophecy, and prophecy, by nature, has a future fulfillment.

The hundreds of prophecies in the Bible that have already been fulfilled took place literally, not figuratively. There is no indication anywhere in Scripture that God suggests we switch to a new method of understanding prophecy. A prophecy is given, then at some point later it is fulfilled, just as described. That is the clear nature and pattern of prophecy.

The futurist view is the only one that interprets Revelation literally—which is the same way we interpret the rest of Scripture. In the passages where we find symbolic language, the answers are provided in the immediate or broader context of Scripture—not from our own subjective ideas. Where figures of speech are used, they are clear statements that were understood by the original audience. The futurist view of Revelation makes the most logical sense, honors God as a clear communicator, uses the same method to interpret all of Scripture consistently, and takes God's Word at face value.

The book of Revelation describes unprecedented supernatural events. Rather than explain them away because they are too hard to believe, we should take God at his Word. I've heard prophecy experts state that the book of Revelation is not hard to understand—it's just hard to believe. But if we believe Genesis

1:1, we should have no problem believing every detail in the book of Revelation will come to pass, just as all earlier Bible prophecies have.

Genesis 1:1—In the beginning God created the heavens and the earth

The Two Basic Approaches

The *idealist*, *preterist*, and *historicist* views all allegorize or spiritualize Scripture in some fashion. Ultimately, by opening the door to allegorical interpretation, these views let the reader come up with meanings that may stray from what the apostle John intended to communicate in Revelation.

The *futurist* view is the only approach that maintains a consistent literal understanding of Scripture from beginning to end. So there are two main categories of interpretive thought: an allegorical interpretation of Scripture, or a literal interpretation of Scripture. For the reasons I stated earlier, I am firmly convinced we are to go with a literal interpretation of Scripture, and that the futurist view is the one that makes the greatest sense.

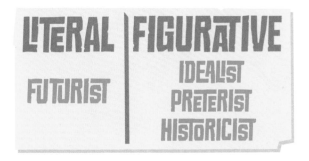

Either Scripture can be spiritualized, with the interpreter deciding which passages have symbolic meaning, or all of Scripture is meant to be taken literally and understood by the plain and clear meanings of the words themselves.

The futurist view of Bible prophecy is the only view that holds to a literal interpretation of Scripture. That means it allows the Bible to speak for itself. I don't trust anyone, including myself, to arbitrarily decide which portions of Scripture can be spiritualized—especially when there is no consistent or logical method for determining when to spiritualize the text.

CHAPTER 6

The Three Views
of the Rapture

The Lord himself will come down from heaven, with a loud command, with the voice of the archangel and with the trumpet call of God, and the dead in Christ will rise first. After that, we who are still alive and are left will be caught up together with them in the clouds to meet the Lord in the air. And so we will be with the Lord forever.

1 THESSALONIANS 4:16-17

I grew up in the Washington, DC metro area, and our family lived close enough to a few modest ski resorts that we would take an occasional day trip or two each winter. One year when I was about 10 years old, my father's office organized a President's Day weekend trip to a large ski resort near Pittsburgh, Pennsylvania. It's wasn't Breckenridge, but it was impressive as far as East Coast ski resorts go.

My siblings and I learned about the trip months in advance. My sister was still a bit too young to appreciate the splendor of the upcoming expedition, but my stepbrothers and I could barely wait. We pored over the brochures. We tried on our ski gloves, goggles, and the obnoxiously bright orange ski outfits we received on Christmas. We carefully planned our days and mapped out all the slopes we wanted to tackle.

We discovered from the brochures that on the outside chance we grew tired of skiing, we could retreat into the warmth and comfort of the resort and continue our adventure indoors. There we would find all-you-can-eat buffets, an indoor swimming pool, a bowling alley, a sprawling arcade, and even a roller-skating rink. This seemed like heaven on earth, and our anticipation grew as we drew closer to the moment when we would finally step foot on the idling charter bus—bound for snowy Pennsylvania.

For believers in Jesus Christ, there lies before us a guaranteed future event that should ignite an excitement and passion greater than any vacation, trip, or earthly adventure ever could. As the centuries, years, and months of the church age continue to tick by, we should grow in anticipation of a supernatural event that we are destined for—the instantaneous catching away of all true believers in Christ. It is the next thing on the prophetic event calendar and it is an imminent one, meaning there are no preconditions that must take place for it to occur. It could happen at any moment.

This Navy-SEALs-like rescue operation is known as the rapture. One of our enemy's titles is "the prince of the power of the air" (Ephesians 2:2 NKJV). Based on the verse at the chapter opening, Jesus himself will invade the enemy's territory and whisk away his bride—the church—from right under Satan's nose.

QUICK FACT: DID YOU KNOW...
that the "S-E-A-L" in Navy SEALS stands for
SEA, AIR, AND LAND?

Generations of believers have longed to be alive when this worldwide supernatural event occurs. We don't know if we are that generation, but one thing is for sure: We have more reason to believe we are closer to the rapture than any other generation in history. First, because with every second that passes, we draw closer chronologically to this guaranteed future event. And second, because all the biblical signs and conditions pointing to the tribulation are forming in our day. If the rapture occurs prior to the tribulation, and we're seeing the signs pointing to the tribulation period, then the rapture must be drawing close. To use a common analogy, if we see signs of Christmas around us, then we know that Thanksgiving must be near. These end-time signs and conditions have never been so thoroughly in place for any other generation—more on that beginning in chapter 14.

If you have ever been confused about the rapture or if you have wondered about its significance, please read this chapter carefully. As believers in Christ, it is vital for us to have a clear understanding of this faith-anchoring event.

The Promises from Jesus

In John chapter 14, Jesus sheds light on this event along with a promise to return, and a promise to take us with him. He said in verses 2-3, "In My Father's house are many mansions; if it were not so, I would have told you. I go to prepare a place for you. And if I go and prepare a place for you, I will come again and receive you to Myself; that where I am, there you may be also" (NKJV).

At first glance, this may not seem relevant to the topic at hand. The rapture was a mystery until Paul, inspired by the Holy Spirit, wrote down the revelation he had received concerning the event. But if we compare Jesus's statements in this passage with Paul's statements from the key rapture text cited at the beginning of this chapter, we find an amazing correlation between the two. This confirms the two passages are talking about the same event.

THE RAPTURE ACCORDING TO PAUL & JESUS

1 THESSALONIANS 4:16-17	JOHN 14:3
For the Lord himself will come down from heaven,	And if I go and prepare a place for you,
...the dead in Christ will rise first. After that, we who are still alive and are left will be caught up together with them in the clouds to meet the Lord in the air.	I will come back and take you to be with me
And so we will be with the Lord forever.	that you also may be where I am.

We're given two promises in John 14:2-3: (1) that Jesus himself is leaving to go and prepare a place for us, and (2) that he is going to come again and receive us to himself. Let's take a closer look at these promises:

Going to Prepare a Place

Scripture tells us that all of creation was made through Jesus. He was also a carpenter by trade before he began his earthly ministry. If it took him only six days to create the heavens and the earth, can you imagine how amazing *our* future place is going to be? What meticulous care and attention to personal detail must be given to something that takes Jesus 2,000 years to build?

> John 1:3—Through him all things were made; without him nothing was made that has been made.

Coming Back to Receive Us

Second, Jesus promised that he is coming back to receive us. He's not just coming back *to* us. He's also *receiving* us—that is, we're going to him. In other words, he's meeting us somewhere in the middle. In 1 Thessalonians 4 we are given more information about this, as well as the exact order of events for the rapture.

Order of Events

The subevents of the rapture will likely happen in extremely quick succession—some perhaps simultaneously.

First, the Lord himself will come down with a shout. Will he shout, "Come forth!" as he did when he raised his friend Lazarus from the dead? Will he shout, "Come up here!" like he did with John in Revelation chapter 4? We can only speculate, but I believe Christians will hear his unmistakable shout as he suddenly cracks open our plane of existence somewhere in the sky—right in the heart of the enemy's territory.

Second, we will hear the voice of the archangel. This is probably the archangel Michael, who leads God's armies against Satan's forces in Revelation and is specifically referenced in the book of Jude. We also find him in the Old Testament book of Daniel battling against regional fallen angels so he can get a critical prophetic message from God to Daniel.

Michael is God's top general, perhaps the same rank or slightly lower than the rank Satan had before he rebelled against God. This shout is likely a war cry given as the enemy's territory is invaded. It could also be the announcement of the groom (Jesus) coming to fetch his bride (the church), as was the custom in ancient Jewish wedding traditions. Or, perhaps it is both.

THE 5 EVENTS OF THE RAPTURE

1. Lord comes down with a shout
2. voice of the archangel is heard
3. the trumpet of God is heard
4. rapture of dead church-age believers
5. rapture of all living believers

Third, we will hear the trumpet of God—the shofar—a distinctive blowing of a horn to call people to battle or to assemble for an important meeting or celebration. Both uses are applicable here.

Fourth, the dead in Christ will rise. This is the long-promised resurrection. What the Bible refers to as the *first resurrection* and the rapture are the same event. Those church-age believers who have already died will receive their glorified bodies fit for heaven.

Fifth and finally, this passage tells us that we who are still alive will be caught up with the other church-age believers to meet the Lord in the air. Just as believers who are resurrected from the dead will receive bodies fit for heaven, we who are alive will also be instantly changed into new bodies. Can you imagine the joy as living believers are reunited with loved ones who preceded them in death, and they are all standing together before the Lord Jesus Christ in all of his glory?

1 Corinthians 15:51-53—Listen, I tell you a mystery: We will not all sleep, but we will all be changed—in a flash, in the twinkling of an eye, at the last trumpet. For the trumpet will sound, the dead will be raised imperishable, and we will be changed. For the perishable must clothe itself with the imperishable, and the mortal with immortality.

What can be more exciting than this? One generation of Christians will not see death. Instead, they will be changed and snatched up to God's throne in a millisecond and will remain with the Lord forever. It is possible that we are that generation.

What about you? What comes to mind when you think about the rapture? Instead of excitement and joy, many experience fear, apathy, or confusion. In Titus 2:13, Paul said we should be looking for the rapture, and he called it "the blessed hope." The problem is we have an enemy who wants to steal our hope and blur our understanding of this momentous event. The only way to fight his strategy is to look directly at the issue and carefully study what the Bible has to say about it.

Titus 2:13—looking for the blessed hope and glorious appearing of our great God and Savior Jesus Christ (NKJV).

The Three Main Views of the Rapture

The key question to address at this point is this: *When* does the rapture take place in the context of end-time events? If you recall the definitions we looked at earlier, the seven-year tribulation will begin at the end of the church age. During the tribulation, God's wrath will be poured out on the earth, and an evil world ruler known as the antichrist will rise to power and attempt to annihilate the Jews. These will be the worst seven years of history on every conceivable level. We established in the previous chapter that Scripture passages about the end times should be understood literally, not be spiritualized. Given that fact, we can be confident that the clear statements about the rapture, the tribulation period, and the millennial kingdom are not merely figures of speech, but refer to literal future events.

One of the in-house debates among believers who take God's Word literally concerns the timing of the rapture in relation to the tribulation period. An understanding of the three major views is essential so you can study Scripture and form your own convictions. These three points of view are the pre-tribulation rapture view, the mid-tribulation rapture view, and the post-tribulation rapture view. Whole books have been written on this debate, but for now, it's sufficient to look at the basics of each view, along with their key strengths and weaknesses.

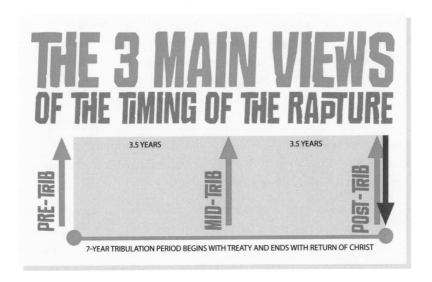

The Pre-Tribulation View

This view teaches that the rapture will occur *before* the seven-year tribulation period. This is the view I hold. The overwhelming strengths for this view are highlighted in the next chapter. The only struggle at all with this view is that there is no single clear chronological description in Scripture that provides the exact order of all end-time events. This weakness exists in all three views, however, and is the reason all relevant passages need to be studied so you can build a properly interpreted viewpoint. Where Scripture is silent we should be too; but where it provides information, we must not overlook it.

The Mid-Tribulation View

This view states that the rapture will occur at the middle of the seven-year tribulation period. Some of the arguments for this position are as follows.

There are several verses that mention key events that will occur at the midpoint of the tribulation, such as the defilement of the temple and the beginning of terrible persecution of the Jewish people. There are also verses that make it clear that the second half of the tribulation will be worse than the first half. It is at the midpoint of the tribulation that people will be forced to accept or reject the mark of the beast, and anyone who rejects it will be killed.

Proponents of the mid-trib view assert that the events of the first 3.5 years of the tribulation reflect man's wrath against man, not God's wrath upon mankind. They also cite that the *two witnesses* of Revelation chapter 11 are raptured at the midpoint of the tribulation. They assert that this rapture of the two witnesses will also include the worldwide rapture of the church.

Mid-tribulation proponents also equate the trumpet mentioned in 1 Thessalonians 4:16 (see verse at the beginning of this chapter) with the last of the trumpet judgments in the book of Revelation, which indeed take place during the second half of the tribulation period.

This view is, I believe, the second strongest of the three—but a very distant second for the reasons I'll cite in the next chapter. It's true that the tribulation is split into two periods of 3.5 years and that the worst persecution will occur during the second half, particularly for the Jewish people. However, it is also clear that God's wrath will be poured out during the first half. In Revelation chapter 6, at the beginning of the tribulation, the events taking place are specifically described as "the great day of their wrath" (verse 17). The first judgments are the Seal Judgments, and Jesus is the one who opens the judgments, not man. This is the long-prophesied *Day of the Lord* foretold by the major and minor prophets of the Old Testament.

> Revelation 6:17—For the great day of their wrath has come, and who can withstand it?

Here is a *partial* list of what will occur during the first half of the tribulation: world war, global famine, worldwide pandemic, earthquakes so severe that mountains are leveled and islands disappear, massive meteor showers, one-third of the earth and all of the grass burned up, one-third of the sea turned into blood, one-third of sea life killed, a very large meteor strike that makes the water in one-third of the rivers undrinkable, another large meteor that cracks the earth's crust, demonic locusts, one-third of mankind killed, and the two witnesses (probably Elijah and Moses) breathing fire on their enemies and holding back the rain so drought conditions occur. As you can see, the first half of the tribulation is no cakewalk. Nor are the events all a result of man's wrath. These are divine judgments.

While it is true that the two witnesses will be raptured after they are killed and resurrected, there is no indication that anyone else on earth will be raptured at that time. In fact, there are other mini-raptures of individuals in both the Old and New Testaments. By contrast, the rapture described in 1 Thessalonians 4 clearly includes all true believers.

The mid-tribulation argument that the reference to "the last trumpet" is pointing to the trumpet judgments is not a strong one because the chronology is off. The two witnesses are raptured in verse 12 of Revelation 11, but the last trumpet judgments don't occur until verse 15.

In 1 Corinthians 15:52, the reference to believers being changed in the twinkling of an eye at the sound of the last trumpet is not talking about the trumpet judgments during the tribulation. In Jewish culture, trumpets were blown to mark the beginning and end of events. This verse is pointing to the fact that the church age, or age of grace, is coming to an end and a new era or dispensation (the tribulation, then the kingdom) is about to begin. It is the last trumpet of the church age.

> 1 Corinthians 15:52—In a flash, in the twinkling of an eye, at the last trumpet. For the trumpet will sound, the dead will be raised imperishable, and we will be changed.

The Post-Tribulation View

This view states that the rapture will occur at the end of the seven-year tribulation period simultaneous with the second coming of Jesus. So this view asserts that the few Christians who are still alive on earth at Christ's return will be raptured up with Jesus in the clouds, then will immediately come right back down with him to the earth again.

One of the main arguments for this view is that Revelation talks about saints being on the earth during the tribulation period. Proponents say that if it were true that all Christians are raptured prior to the tribulation, then there would be no saints to speak of during the tribulation.

But we understand from Revelation that during the tribulation there will be 144,000 Jewish evangelists and an angel who preach the gospel to the entire world. Millions of people who heard the gospel prior to the rapture, but for whatever reason didn't respond, will surely turn to Jesus and be saved once they see the rapture take place. Scripture is clear that post-rapture conditions on earth will force everyone to make a decision one way or the other. Many will choose Christ, and many will choose against him. As supernatural events suddenly burst onto the global scene beginning with the rapture, there will no longer be any middle ground. The world will choose sides.

One of the strongest arguments against the post-trib view is that the rapture is seen as an imminent or anytime event for which no one knows the day or the hour. We are told that Jesus will come like a thief in the night. In contrast, Christ's actual return to earth will occur exactly at the end of the seven-year tribulation period, which, according to Daniel 9:27, officially begins with the signing of a seven-year peace treaty between Israel and her neighbors. This treaty will be brokered by the antichrist.

If the post-trib view that the rapture will occur at Christ's return were correct, then any Scripture passages about the day and hour of his return being unknown would no longer be accurate. It would not be possible to say that Christ's coming will be a surprise, or that he "will come like a thief in the night" (1 Thessalonians 5:12).

> 1 Thessalonians 5:2—for you know very well that the day of the Lord will come like a thief in the night.

Pre-Trib Strengths?

"What are the strengths of the pre-tribulation rapture position?" you ask. The whole next chapter addresses this question. Please read on. You're in for an exciting and encouraging ride!

CHAPTER 7

Five Reasons to Believe in the Pre-Tribulation View of the Rapture

...the appearing of the glory of our great God and Savior, Jesus Christ.

TITUS 2:13

My wife loves watching documentary crime shows about tough cases that are eventually solved through the effective use of forensic science. Some episodes feature new technology used to solve cold cases, while other episodes highlight new forensic methods developed to solve tough cases or prove a suspect's guilt or innocence.

In each episode, science and logic come together to solve a murder case and construct an accurate picture of the timeline and details of the crime. The stories of the voiceless victims are told by the forensic evidence left behind.

Speaking of left behind—that was the title of the first book in the popular 1990s Left Behind series written by Tim LaHaye and Jerry B. Jenkins. The 16 books in the series were all bestsellers, and the unique feature of the series was that the books were written as novels. The theology and chronology of end-time events were woven into a powerful narrative using well-developed characters whom readers identified with.

"So, what's the connection between forensics and *Left Behind*?" you ask. The Left Behind series was written from a thoroughly pre-trib point of view. At the time when the first book was released, I had read the book of Revelation a few times and even worked through a deductive study guide on the book, but I wasn't able to see how someone like Tim LaHaye could be so dogmatic about the order and nature of end-time events. You could say that at that time I held a "pan-trib" view. I knew it would all pan out in the end, but didn't see any crystal-clear order of events that I could be dogmatic about, though I leaned toward the pre-trib view.

Tim LaHaye's bold convictions and clear explanations about the end-times drove me to study the topic more in depth. What I learned was that the book of Revelation was only part of the puzzle. Its mystery is solved by studying it alongside certain books in the Old Testament, particularly the major and minor prophets. I discovered that the Old Testament lays the foundation that the book of Revelation is built upon.

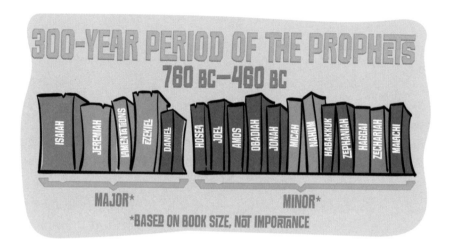

Forensics is to a crime scene what cross-referenced Bible study is to understanding end-time events. Students of the Bible must carefully look at all the available details and use logic to form conclusions and understand the big picture. Isaiah 28:9-10 aptly explains the care and detail we must use in developing theology and convictions. It tells us, "Precept must be upon precept, precept upon precept, line upon line, line upon line, here a little, there a little" (NKJV).

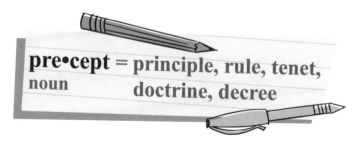

What blew me away personally was that simple fact that the more I studied the details, the more I saw how they fit together precisely like the pieces of a puzzle—even though those details were written by many different men across many different time periods.

As I began to systematically study Scripture to form my own perspectives about end-time events, I found that logic and the forensics of Bible study began to build my end-time framework one brick or puzzle piece at a time—line upon line, precept upon precept. The point I'm making here is that a careful study *will* paint a clear picture of key end-time events and chronology—not for every detail, but definitely for the broader brushstrokes.

Over time, my forensics-style study of prophecy taught me that there are many biblical reasons to believe in the pre-tribulation position. Entire books have been written on the subject, but for the purposes of this study, I have chosen to present what I believe are the five most compelling reasons for holding this view. But don't take my word for it. Become a Bible forensics expert yourself and let this drive you to a deeper study of your own. I promise that when you take the time to do careful study, you will discover great treasures along the way.

Reasons for a Pre-Tribulation Rapture
Reason #1: We Are Not Appointed to Wrath

One key reason the rapture must occur prior to the beginning of the tribulation period is that several verses in the Bible explicitly state that believers in Christ are not appointed to wrath. The seven-year tribulation period increases in severity as various judgments are poured out, and the last 3.5 years are clearly the worst of the worst. But the entire seven-year period is a display of God's wrath.

> Zephaniah 1:15—That day will be a day of wrath— a day of distress and anguish, a day of trouble and ruin, a day of darkness and gloom, a day of clouds and blackness.

We can see, for example, that early in the tribulation period, those who experience the seal judgments describe them as God's wrath. In Revelation chapter 6, where the judgments begin, we find the ruling elite hiding underground and in caves. In verses 16 and 17 we read, "They called to the mountains and the rocks, 'Fall on us and hide us from the face of him who sits on the throne and from the *wrath of the Lamb!* For the *great day of their wrath has come,* and who can withstand it?'" (emphasis added)

Eight Old Testament prophets prophesy about a future *Day of the Lord,* a term that refers to the tribulation period as a clear and deliberate manifestation of God's wrath against evil. The phrase is used 19 times in the Old Testament and, in every single case, the ultimate fulfillment is a time during which God finally pours out his wrath on a sinful world.

The term *Day of the Lord* is used five times in the New Testament and must be seen in light of the Old Testament texts. Currently we are living in the *age of grace,* but the *Day of the Lord* will be a seven-year period of judgment and wrath.

FOR FURTHER STUDY:
OLD TESTAMENT USES OF THE DAY OF THE LORD

Isaiah 2:12; 13:6, 9   Obadiah 15
Ezekiel 13:5; 30:3   Zephaniah 1:7, 14
Joel 1:15; 2:1, 11, 31; 3:14 Zechariah 14:1
Amos 5:18, 20   Malachi 4:5

In 1 Thessalonians 5, Paul addressed the Day of the Lord because some believers from this young church were concerned that they may have to go through it. Paul wrote 11 verses to clear up the matter, and in 1 Thessalonians 5:9 he said, in clear terms, "God did not appoint us to suffer wrath but to receive salvation through our Lord Jesus Christ."

Then in verse 10, Paul further drove the point home by reminding the believers that whether they were awake or asleep (alive or dead) at the time of this event, they would live together with Christ. Then he said in verse 11, "Therefore encourage one another." Here's the Todd's-paraphrase-version of this passage: "God never planned for you to go through the Day of the Lord, and somehow he will keep you out of it—even if you are still alive when it's about to start. So, encourage each other with the fact that you won't experience this terrible time."

Our salvation has three applications: a past, a present, and a future. We are saved from the *penalty* of our sin when we accept Christ (past); we are being saved from the *power* of sin as we grow spiritually (present); and we will be saved from the very *presence* of sin and God's wrath when we meet the Lord in death or by rapture (future). The people Paul was addressing already knew they were saved from the penalty of sin. It's clear that the salvation Paul was talking about in 1 Thessalonians 5:9 was their ultimate salvation, or when they will stand in the presence of their Lord.

Here are a few more verses that support the fact that church-age Christians will not experience God's wrath during the tribulation period:

> Romans 5:9— "Since we have now been justified by his blood, how much more shall we be *saved from God's wrath* through him!"
>
> 1 Thessalonians 1:10—"...to wait for his Son from heaven, whom he raised from the dead—Jesus, who *rescues us from the coming wrath.*"
>
> Revelation 3:10—"Because you have kept My command to persevere, *I also will keep you from the hour of trial which shall come upon the whole world*, to test those who dwell on the earth" (NKJV).

Notice in Revelation 3:10 that God will keep the whole church *from* (not through) the *hour* of trial (a specific event/time frame), which will come upon the *whole* world (this is a global judgment).

Reason #2: Patterns and Types

Scripture tells us in Hebrews 13:8 that "Jesus Christ is the same yesterday and today and forever." In the pages of the Bible, we discover a God of character and consistency. We learn about his nature through his words and actions. We can analyze Old Testament examples of God's judgment to gain insight into the future judgment of the tribulation period.

Patterns of God's judgment are seen clearly in the events related to Noah's flood in Genesis 6–8, the destruction of Sodom and Gomorrah in Genesis 18–19, and the averted judgment of Nineveh in the book of Jonah.

In the example of the flood, the world was corrupt except for righteous Noah and his family. God warned Noah of the coming judgment and gave him instructions on how to be saved. After constructing the ark, Noah and his family were preserved in it after God himself closed the doors *seven days* before the earth's destruction by the flood.

As the giant springs of the deep from below and the deluge from above brought global destruction, Noah and his family were kept high above God's judgment. After the period of judgment was over, Noah and his family came down upon the earth to begin a new era of history.

We see the striking parallels with end-time events, during which the church will be raptured and kept safe high above the judgments taking place on earth during the seven years of the tribulation, after which the church will return with Christ to initiate a new era—the millennial kingdom.

In the example of Sodom and Gomorrah, Lot and his family were forcefully taken out of the city that was in the low-lying plain, and told to go to the mountains to avert God's judgment. As I stated in a previous chapter, the word *harpazo*, which translates to "the rapture," carries with it the idea of a sudden and forceful snatching away as we are *caught up* to meet the Lord in the air prior to the wrath of God coming upon the earth.

In the example of Nineveh, Jonah was told to warn the evil people of that city to repent or be destroyed by God's judgment. After delivering his message, Jonah sat at a distance and waited for judgment to fall. The difference here was that the people of Nineveh actually did repent, so God's judgment didn't come upon that generation of Ninevites. What a beautiful reminder to us that God always provides a way to escape his judgment even for the worst offenders if they would just heed his warning and turn to him for salvation.

There are many other examples of this in the Bible. Daniel taken up to a *higher* position of authority just before his three friends Shadrach, Meshach, and Abednego were thrown into the fiery furnace heated seven times—there's that number again—hotter than normal. Rahab the prostitute was kept safe in her home with the red rope in the window of Jericho's upper wall while the entire city below was destroyed supernaturally by God. Before the divine destruction, Joshua and the Israelite army marched around the city for seven days, and on the seventh day, they marched seven times around the city. Then a trumpet blast went forth, and the city walls fell supernaturally.

Those examples show God's consistent pattern of patience, warning, removal of the righteous, then finally, judgment. We also see the clear pattern of the number seven again and again. We are told multiple times in Scripture that God is *slow to anger* (Exodus 34:6; Numbers 14:18; Nehemiah 9:17; Psalm 86:15; Joel 2:13; Jonah 4:2; Nahum 1:3). He doesn't want to send judgment, but he must if he is God. Second Peter 3:9 tells us that "the Lord is not slow in keeping his promise, as some understand slowness. Instead he is patient with you, *not wanting anyone to perish*, but everyone to come to repentance" (emphasis added).

Reason #3: The Jewish Wedding Tradition

If you read about the Jewish wedding traditions that were in place at the time of Christ and the writing of the New Testament, you'll find that various details of the Jewish wedding process closely resemble the details of Jesus's first coming, the rapture, and his return.

The Jewish wedding tradition had two parts: first was the betrothal or dedication—or what we call the engagement, except in this case it was a legally binding commitment. Then the betrothal was followed by the wedding itself and consummation of the marriage.

The first event in the tradition featured the groom leaving his father's house to travel to his future bride's home. The groom would then pay a great price for the bride. The potential bride would then either accept or reject this offer. If she accepted, then a marriage contract would be written and she would be legally bound and set apart for the groom. The two would drink from a single cup of wine, symbolizing their union.

Next the groom would go back to his father's house for an extended but undetermined amount of time to prepare a home for his bride. When the father determined that everything had been adequately prepared, he would send the son to go and get his bride. The bride would know the general time frame during which to expect the groom, but not the exact day. Then one day a procession of groomsmen blowing shofars would announce the groom's sudden arrival, and the groom would whisk away his waiting bride.

The groom would then take the bride home to the wedding chamber, where they were sealed for seven days. At the end of the seven days they would emerge and enjoy a great wedding feast to commemorate the consummation of their marriage.

JEWISH WEDDING TRADITIONS
AND THE RAPTURE

	BETROTHAL		1ST COMING OF CHRIST
	LEAVE FATHER'S HOUSE	JESUS LEFT HEAVEN	
	TRAVEL TO DESIRED BRIDE'S HOME	CAME TO EARTH AS A BABY	
	PAY A GREAT PRICE FOR THE BRIDE	DIED ON THE CROSS FOR OUR SINS	
	OFFER ACCEPTED OR REJECTED	OFFERS SALVATION TO US	
	MARRIAGE CONTRACT/LEGALLY BOUND TOGETHER	IF WE ACCEPT WE BECOME THE CHURCH ("BRIDE OF CHRIST")	
	GROOM BACK TO FATHER'S HOUSE TO PREPARE HOME	JESUS WENT BACK TO PREPARE A PLACE FOR US	
	FATHER SENDS SON BACK WHEN ALL IS READY	GOD KNOWS THE "DAY AND HOUR" HE WILL SEND THE SON	
WEDDING	GROOMSMEN ANNOUNCE GROOM'S ARRIVAL	THE ARCHANGEL WILL SHOUT AND A TRUMPET WILL BLOW	RAPTURE AND CHURCH IN HEAVEN DURING TRIBULATION PERIOD
	BRIDE IMMEDIATELY TAKEN BACK WITH GROOM	THE CHURCH/BRIDE OF CHRIST WILL BE RAPTURED	
	THE TWO ENTER WEDDING CHAMBER FOR 7 DAYS	THE CHURCH WILL BE IN HEAVEN DURING THE TRIBULATION	
	GREAT WEDDING FEAST AT END OF 7 DAYS	THE CHURCH WILL ATTEND THE WEDDING FEAST OF THE LAMB	

In Scripture, the church is often referred to as the bride and Jesus is depicted as the groom. He left his Father's house, paid a great price for us (the church, also known as the bride of Christ) by dying on the cross, instituted communion for us to observe until he returns, and went back to heaven, where he said he would prepare a place for us.

We are told to keep watch for his return, which will happen suddenly and be announced with trumpets. This return is what's known as the rapture, when we will be taken to be with Christ in heaven before the seven-year tribulation period. At the end of the tribulation, according to Revelation 19, the marriage supper of the Lamb will take place, during which we will celebrate our ultimate union with the Lord.

These end-time events perfectly parallel the Jewish wedding traditions referred to frequently by Jesus and the apostles. Now here is the reason this oft-referenced analogy supports a pre-tribulation rapture: It makes no logical sense for a loving groom to ask for a woman's hand in marriage, then send her out to get beat up by every horrific form of danger imaginable, then return and say, "Hey honey, you ready to get married, consummate our union, and have a great feast?" Even worse, if this were the case, the wrath that the bride would experience would come at the hands of the father of the groom!

This scenario does not line up with Scripture, or what we know about the love and character of God. Both the mid-tribulation and post-tribulation views require the bride to experience the father's wrath for either three-and-a-half or seven years of the worst judgment the planet will ever face.

Reason #4: The Focus of the Tribulation Is Israel, Not the Church

In the book of Revelation, the first three chapters are all about the church. The word "church" is used 19 times in the first three chapters. Then at the beginning of chapter 4 there is a "door standing open in heaven" and a "voice...like a trumpet" tells John to "come up here." The next scene has John standing in heaven's throne room. The church is not seen again in Revelation until chapter 19, when

Christ is about to return to earth with his bride, or the church. The church is also part of the armies of heaven who return with Christ in Revelation 19:14.

As we have already mentioned, in the Old Testament, the tribulation period was known as the Day of the Lord, but it was also referred to as "the time of trouble for Jacob" (Jeremiah 30:7). The 70 weeks of Daniel 9 is 100 percent about God's plan for the Jewish race. As I mentioned, there is a mysterious pause or break between the sixty-ninth and seventieth weeks (of years), which we now know as the church age or the age of grace.

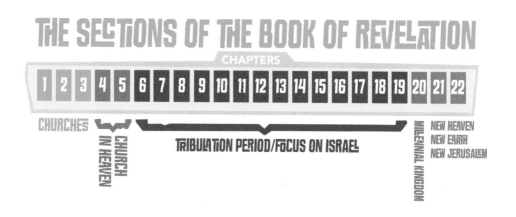

Reason #5: 2 Thessalonians 2

As mentioned earlier under Reason #1, the Thessalonian believers had concerns about the Day of the Lord. Paul addressed their concerns in 1 Thessalonians 5, but less than a year later, the believers in this young church needed more clarity on the topic due to some false reports.

In 2 Thessalonians 2, Paul addressed a hoax that had been spreading, which claimed that the tribulation period had already begun. So he provided a wealth of support for the pre-tribulation position in the first eight verses to set the people's minds at ease.

This is such an important passage it is well worth our time to take a closer look at it:

2 Thessalonians 2:1-8 — Concerning the coming of our Lord Jesus Christ and our being gathered to him, we ask you, brothers and sisters, not to become easily unsettled or alarmed by the teaching allegedly from us —whether by a prophecy or by word of mouth or by letter —asserting that the day of the Lord has already come. Don't let anyone deceive you in any way, for that day will not come until the rebellion occurs and the man of lawlessness is revealed, the man doomed to destruction. He will oppose and will exalt himself over everything that is called God or is worshiped, so that he sets himself up in God's temple, proclaiming himself to be God. Don't you remember that when I was with you I used to tell you these things? And now you know what is holding him back, so that he may be revealed at the proper time. For the secret power of lawlessness is already at work; but the one who now holds it back will continue to do so till he is taken out of the way. And then the lawless one will be revealed, whom the Lord Jesus will overthrow with the breath of his mouth and destroy by the splendor of his coming.

In verse 1, Paul established what he was talking about—the coming of Jesus and our being gathered to him. In other words, *the rapture*. In verse 2, he told the Thessalonian believers not to be alarmed by any reports that the tribulation had started. In verse 3, Paul said the tribulation will not start until certain things happen.

This is where it gets interesting. He plainly said the tribulation would not start until two things happened: (1) the rebellion occurred, and (2) the man of lawlessness was revealed. "Man of lawlessness" is another name for the antichrist. So the rebellion must occur, and the antichrist must be revealed. We know from Daniel 9:27 that it is the antichrist who will confirm a covenant—some type of peace agreement—with Israel for seven years. At the time this treaty is finalized, we will have absolute confirmation about the identity of the antichrist.

But what about "the rebellion" that must occur? Some Bible versions translate this word "apostasy" or "falling away." The Greek word here is *apostasia*, and we have transliterated it into the word *apostasy*. The verb form of this word is *aphistemi*, which means "departure." This can be a spiritual departure or a physical departure, and there is a debate among prophecy teachers about which kind it means.

It is my belief that the context supports a physical departure—in other words, the rapture. Because this passage is talking about a specific event—*the* apostosia—and because Paul opened with a reference to the rapture and concluded with a reference to the rapture, for this to refer to a physical departure works well. If this is accurate, it is the clearest proof of a pre-tribulation rapture.

Churches have been falling away from truth since the first century and continue to do so in our day. So this phrase is either talking about a specific time-bound event that includes a large-scale sudden apostasy of the church, or it is talking about a specific time-bound event that includes a large-scale sudden physical departure of the church. Those are the only two options, and the context favors the latter.

QUICK FACT: DID YOU KNOW...

that Harvard, Yale, Princeton, and Oxford used to be Christian colleges or seminaries?

In verse 6, Paul stated that something is holding back the antichrist, and in verse 7, he said that the thing holding back the antichrist is a person. He said "the one" holding the antichrist back will at some point be "taken out of the way." We know that the Holy Spirit restrains sin, and we know that since the day of Pentecost, the Holy Spirit has indwelt each true believer in Christ. This is true of the Holy Spirit only during the church age. At the moment of the rapture, the church made up of believers—and the Holy Spirit living in them—will literally be "taken out of the way." This will allow evil to break loose like never before and for the world to be deceived by Satan's man who has been waiting in the wings. However imperfect, the church has always had a restraining influence on evil. But that won't be the case after the rapture because the church will be gone.

The Blessed Hope!

All these factors powerfully support a pre-tribulation view of the rapture. The more I study Scripture, the more thoroughly convinced I am that Christians on earth will be raptured prior to the tribulation period. How else could Paul refer to the Lord's coming as "the blessed hope" in Titus 2:13? There's absolutely nothing blessed or hopeful about believers having to go through the tribulation period.

The understanding that our gracious Lord will whisk away the church prior to his wrath being poured out on an ungodly world should give us hope, comfort, joy, and an urgent desire to share our faith with those who don't know Christ.

CHAPTER 8

The Three Views of the Millennium

I saw an angel coming down out of heaven, having the key to the Abyss and holding in his hand a great chain. He seized the dragon, that ancient serpent, who is the devil, or Satan, and bound him for a thousand years. He threw him into the Abyss, and locked and sealed it over him, to keep him from deceiving the nations anymore until the thousand years were ended. After that, he must be set free for a short time.

REVELATION 20:1-3

Soon after becoming a Christian I stumbled across a couple of radio preachers who seemed like they knew their stuff, so I trusted what they said about the end times, not knowing there were other points of view to consider.

My preconceived notion about the Lord's return was very simplistic. I knew Jesus said he was coming back and that there would be a rapture and a final judgment. In my simple thinking, it made sense that these would all occur at the same time. Both of the Bible teachers I heard on the radio were amillennialists who taught that the 1,000-year reign of Christ on earth—which is mentioned five times in seven verses in Revelation chapter 20—was figurative rather than literal, and represented the entire church age.

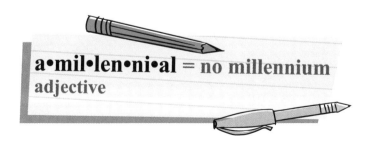

a•mil•len•ni•al = no millennium
adjective

I liked the simple and clean version of having a church age, then the return of Christ to set everything straight, then all believers going to heaven for eternity. Nice and buttoned up. No messy spots. No complexities. But there was a problem. The Word of God kept getting in the way.

Both of the teachers were sincere, but I noticed they both spiritualized various symbols in Revelation differently even though they shared the same end-times view. They also seemed to ignore or illogically explain away any passages of Scripture that contradicted what they taught. For example, I noticed that there seemed to be no indication anywhere in Scripture that the 1,000 years mentioned in Revelation chapter 20 meant anything other than a literal 1,000 years.

I bumped into Old Testament verses that clearly mentioned a future earthly kingdom period during which God himself would rule the world with righteousness (see Isaiah 2:2-4, for example). I also noticed that some people who interacted with Jesus thought he was going to initiate this earthly kingdom at his first coming (remember that the gap we know as the church age was a mystery to them at the time). It bugged me that these radio Bible teachers ignored or explained away any verses that didn't agree with their view.

Acts 1:6—Then they gathered around him and asked him, "Lord, are you at this time going to restore the kingdom to Israel?"

During that season of reading the Bible, I grew to understand that we could either let the Bible speak for itself, or we could insert our own ideas into the text and ignore any verses that got in the way. By this time, I believed the Bible was the *inerrant* word of God and decided to let it speak for itself—even if that meant I had to change some of my convictions. Thankfully, that approach opened up a new world of Bible study and eventually led me to a strong Bible-believing church that held God's Word in high esteem.

in•er•rant = freedom from

verb   **error or untruths**

I share that portion of my journey with you as an example and a challenge. We are all works in progress and should be patient with others—and ourselves—as we study Scripture to form our convictions. Here's the challenge: If you believe the Bible is inspired by God and without error, then let it speak for itself. Don't rest until you are confident you have considered all of the verses related to the theological topic you are studying.

Be open to changing your position if you can't reconcile it with all related Scripture passages. Here's the thing: It's okay to change positions on peripheral issues. At the moment of salvation, we don't know everything in the Bible. It only makes sense that as we learn more, we will refine our understanding and form new convictions.

The Three Views

With that in mind, let's take a look at the various views concerning the millennium and what the Bible has to say. The millennium is the 1,000-year period mentioned in Revelation chapter 20. The three main views are amillennialism, postmillennialism, and premillennialism. Let's take a look at what each view says.

THE 3 VIEWS
OF THE MILLENNIUM

AMILLENNIALISM

POSTMILLENNIALISM

PREMILLENNIALISM

Amillennialism

As mentioned earlier, those who hold this view do not believe in a literal 1,000-year reign of Christ on earth. They teach that the millennium is merely a symbol of the entire church age and that Jesus will return at the very end of it. Regarding the tribulation period, amillennialists are *idealists* or *preterists,* which means they either spiritualize the tribulation events in Revelation to mean various things (idealism), or that the tribulation events described in Revelation all took place primarily in the first century AD (preterism). Amillennialism was first introduced around AD 190 by the Alexandrian school of thought and became the dominant view from the fifth century until the mid-1800s.

Postmillennialism

Postmillennialists spiritualize or allegorize the 1,000 years of Revelation 20 and teach that it represents the church age as Christianity spreads God's kingdom on earth. Those who hold this view believe that the church will Christianize the world, making it the kingdom of God, and that this golden age will usher in the second coming of Jesus. *Postmillennialism* means "after the millennium," and teaches that Jesus will come after the millennium.

Like amillennialists, postmillennialists also believe the tribulation period is symbolic of trials and events during the church age or that they are all past events.

Postmillennialism first appeared as a formalized view in the mid-1600s and grew in popularity particularly during the 1800s and early 1900s as Christianity spread and as the Enlightenment brought advancements in science, medicine, politics, and diplomacy. This progress painted a picture of a hopeful future—until two world wars and the cold war era forced an unwelcome dose of reality on people and negatively impacted the popularity of this view.

Premillennialism

Premillennialists believe that the tribulation is a literal seven-year period of God's judgment that will occur just prior to a literal 1,000-year reign of Christ on earth, as mentioned in Revelation 20. Premillennialism was the view held by the early church up until the third century, and it found a resurgence in the centuries after the Reformation—particularly during the past 150-200 years. Premillennialism is the only one of the three views that approaches Bible prophecy using a literal interpretation method.

In my opinion, this is the strongest and clearest understanding of the 1,000-year period mentioned in Revelation 20. It permits a literal interpretation of Scripture, works in logical tandem with Old Testament prophecies about the earthly kingdom, and supports the fact that God keeps his promises. So why, then, did this view all but disappear during the Middle Ages? Let's take a brief trip through church history to find out.

A Quick History Lesson

Once amillennialism became the official position of the Catholic Church in the third century, it remained the predominant view through the Dark Ages, when Bibles were available only in Latin, chained to pulpits, and used exclusively by priests. With the Reformation (beginning in 1517 with Martin Luther's publication of the "95 Theses") and the invention of the printing press came a series of events that made the Bible accessible to the average person. For the first time in hundreds of years, people other than clergy could study Scripture for themselves.

During this time period there was no official nation of Israel, and the Jewish people were spread all over the world. Very few of them—if any—were Christians. Although Scripture was once again being studied by the common people, which resulted in the discarding of many unbiblical teachings, some errors continued to persist. For example, one theological error some people still held to was the doctrine of *supersessionism*—the belief that the church has *replaced* or *succeeded* the people of Israel in God's plan. This is also known as *replacement theology.*

During the decades following the Reformation period, many people began to gravitate toward a more literal interpretation of Scripture. For example, in the 1600s and 1700s the Puritans of England and New England began to interpret prophecy literally. This resulted in their belief that Jewish people would return to their homeland before the second coming of Jesus. The Puritans prayed regularly for this to happen so that prophecy would be fulfilled.

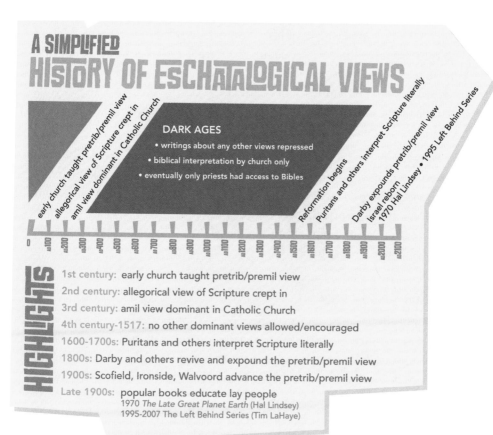

A SIMPLIFIED HISTORY OF ESCHATALOGICAL VIEWS

early church taught pretrib/premil view
allegorical view of Scripture crept in
amil view dominant in Catholic Church

DARK AGES
- writings about any other views repressed
- biblical interpretation by church only
- eventually only priests had access to Bibles

Reformation begins
Puritans and others interpret Scripture literally
Darby expounds pretrib/premil view
Israel reborn
1970 Hal Lindsey • 1995 Left Behind Series

0 AD100 AD200 AD300 AD400 AD500 AD600 AD700 AD800 AD900 AD1000 AD1100 AD1200 AD1300 AD1400 AD1500 AD1600 AD1700 AD1800 AD1900 AD2000 AD2100

HIGHLIGHTS

1st century: early church taught pretrib/premil view
2nd century: allegorical view of Scripture crept in
3rd century: amil view dominant in Catholic Church
4th century-1517: no other dominant views allowed/encouraged
1600-1700s: Puritans and others interpret Scripture literally
1800s: Darby and others revive and expound the pretrib/premil view
1900s: Scofield, Ironside, Walvoord advance the pretrib/premil view
Late 1900s: popular books educate lay people
1970 *The Late Great Planet Earth* (Hal Lindsey)
1995-2007 *The Left Behind Series* (Tim LaHaye)

In the 1830s, Bible teacher John Nelson Darby led an even more formalized theological movement back toward a literal approach to interpreting the Bible. He, and others who picked up on his methods, taught the future fulfillment of Bible prophecy, premillennialism, and a pre-tribulation rapture—all of these the result of adhering to a literal interpretation of Scripture.

This revived concept of taking Scripture at face value became even stronger in the late 1800s and the first half of the 1900s as prophecy students began seeing prophecy fulfilled in real time, including the long-prophesied rebirth of Israel in 1948.

KEY DATES
FOR THE REBIRTH OF ISRAEL

- 1897 Theodor Herzl
  First Zionist Congress in Switzerland

- 1917 Balfour Declaration
  British government supported a Jewish homeland

- 1947 UN Resolution 181
  adopted a plan for a new state of Israel

- May 14, 1948 Israel
  officially became a nation again

This literal fulfillment of prophecy is the greatest proof that we should also expect to see future prophecy about the last days and Jesus's second coming fulfilled in a literal way. This approach to Scripture demands that we take Revelation 20 at face value and understand the millennium to be a literal 1,000-year reign of Christ on earth following a literal seven-year tribulation period. For these reasons, we can be confident that the premillennial view allows for a correct interpretation of Revelation as well as a correct interpretation of various passages in the Old Testament that predict a future earthly kingdom.

CHAPTER 9

The Keys to Watching God's Plan Unfold

I have become its servant by the commission God gave me to present to you the word of God in its fullness—the mystery that has been kept hidden for ages and generations, but is now disclosed to the Lord's people.

COLOSSIANS 1:25-26

I love movies that don't follow common formulas. You know, the kind where the director uses an audience's conditioned expectations against them to build in plot twists and other unexpected features that catch them off guard. A good director will foreshadow key events in veiled language and symbolism to add depth to the story narrative. Well-made movies are worth watching several times because with each viewing you notice new details, connections, and layers of meaning. These devices add to the depth of story and make the intelligent construction even more compelling.

The Bible is written in such a way. The more you study it, the more you see its intentional design and layers of truth hidden in plain sight. Minute details and overlooked passages form a supernatural cohesiveness to the Bible as seemingly unrelated texts fit together intricately. The Hebrew, Aramaic (Old Testament), and Greek (New Testament) languages are incredibly rich with nuances and levels of meaning that add depth and clarity to each verse of Scripture. Jewish rabbis teach that there are 70 levels of understanding when it comes to Scripture. They call this "The Seventy Faces of Torah." These Jewish sages highlight four primary categories of understanding: the literal, the hint, the insight, and the mystery.

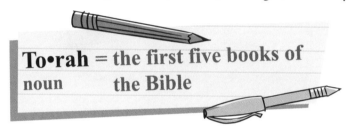

To•rah = the first five books of

noun the Bible

In Part 3 of this book we will study all the fundamental end-times Bible prophecy passages, but first there are a few principles that are important for us to understand. Viewing passages of Scripture in their original context is vital to the study of eschatology. Knowing who the immediate audience was, what the key events were at the time of the writing, what events had occurred prior to the immediate context, when the prophecy was given, and why God was communicating with his people are all important to understanding the prophetic framework. So let's take a look at some big-picture concepts that will help frame our approach to studying key passages of Bible prophecy.

Progressive Revelation
The Unfolding of God's Plan

Today, we have the advantage of holding the complete Word of God in our hands. We have a bound book, or even an app on our cell phone, containing all of God's Word from Genesis to Revelation—the complete record of God's plan from the beginning of creation to the end of the world as we know it. With the flipping

of a few pages we can span thousands of years of biblical history and divine revelation.

Past generations did not have this rich blessing. In previous eras, God's people had to rely on what he had revealed up to that point in history. For example, Adam and Eve had no Scripture, but they had the veiled promise in Genesis 3:15 of a coming Savior. Job had no Scripture and lived about 650 years before Moses received the law. Abraham had God's promise. Moses had a burning-bush experience and face-to-face encounters with God on Mount Sinai. Later the Jewish prophets were given dreams and visions about the nation's destruction and captivity along with promises of restoration and details about a coming Savior. You get the point.

> Genesis 3:15—I will put enmity between you and the woman, and between your offspring and hers; he will crush your head, and you will strike his heel.

> Job 38:32—Can you lead forth the Mazzaroth in their season, or can you guide the Bear with its children? (ESV).

Progressive revelation means that God's revelation to mankind was given in stages. The Old Testament is incomplete without the New Testament. The New Testament is not properly understood without the foundation of the Old Testament. If you study the Bible chronologically, you can pick any area of theology and track how it was revealed progressively over time as God's plan unfolded. Each track of theology has a *Genesis 3:15 moment* that progresses to a *John 3:16 moment,* so to speak. Each revealed hint of God's plan builds throughout Scripture then crescendos in systematic clarity.

> John 3:16—For God so loved the world that he gave his one and only Son, that whoever believes in him shall not perish but have eternal life.

The Different Dispensations

Piece by piece, God's people have built their faith on what they knew up to that point in biblical history. God's will, plan, and character have been revealed to his people progressively over time in different eras or dispensations. The word *dispensation* is used several times in the New Testament, and it means "economy" or "administration." It's a specific way something works in a given context.

For example, when a new president is inaugurated, our country comes under a new administration. Things change. The historical foundation is still the same, but the new administration has different purposes and does things in a different way. Such is the case with each successive biblical administration or dispensation.

A study of Scripture that abides by a literal method of interpretation supports seven distinct dispensations of divine administration.

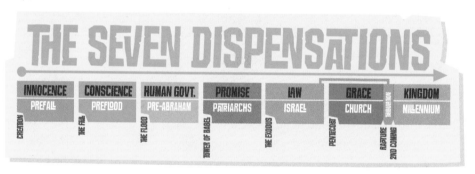

In each dispensation, salvation comes by grace through faith, but the context is different. The principles of God are eternal, but the ways they are administered change from one era to the next. These eras are progressive by nature as each dispensation builds the necessary conditions for the next one.

A basic understanding of dispensations is important in the study of Bible prophecy because certain prophecies apply to certain dispensations and have a purpose that makes sense in the context of that particular dispensation. For example, if you will recall from the last chapter, the future seven-year tribulation period is Daniel's seventieth week (from Daniel chapter 9). Daniel lived in the *dispensation of law*, which focused on God's plan for the Jewish people. The church will be raptured prior to Daniel's seventieth week, and the primary purpose of the tribulation period is to turn the people of Israel back to their true Savior—which Revelation tells us will happen at the end of the tribulation.

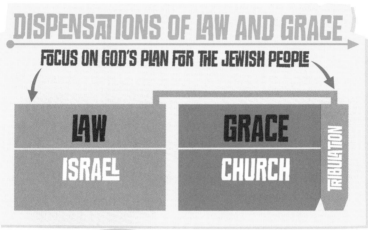

THEODOR HERZL
1860-1904

The First Zionist Congress, led by Theodor Herzl in 1897, was the first official historical milestone toward the rebirth of Israel as foretold in Scripture.

Progressive Illumination

We all know the thrill that comes from understanding a Bible verse for the first time. Or, have you ever studied a passage that you had previously read several times, and suddenly realized a new truth or key fact you never noticed before? That is what happens when the Holy Spirit illuminates God's Word.

Progressive revelation has to do with God's work as he gradually revealed his plans to his people as the Bible was written. Progressive illumination has to do with the Holy Spirit's work of illuminating what is already in God's Word to his people. Consider, for example, Daniel chapter 12. In that passage, Daniel was told twice that some of his most important prophecies would not be understood until the time of the end.

> Daniel 12:4—"You, Daniel, shut up the words, and seal the book until the time of the end; many shall run to and fro, and knowledge shall increase" (NKJV).
>
> Daniel 12:9—He said, "Go your way, Daniel, for the words are closed up and sealed till the time of the end" (NKJV).

Interestingly, the church went through a long period of time with little understanding of what was meant in Daniel 12:4 about the last days being characterized by a great increase in travel and knowledge. But today, Daniel 12:4 makes tremendous sense. Consider this: The first full-scale working railway steam locomotive was built in 1804. So, up until just over 200 years ago, the fastest we could travel was at the speed of a horse galloping. The world record for horse speed is 55 miles per hour. Today a Boeing 747 passenger jet has a cruising speed of 600 miles per hour, and the X-15 military jet flies at 4,520 miles per hour—almost seven times the speed of sound. We have clearly entered the era of increase in travel.

As for knowledge, if everything we knew up until 1900 equaled one inch, then what we have learned from 1900 to the year 2000 would stand as tall as the Washington Monument. This explosion of knowledge has only increased in the twenty-first century. Today nanotechnology knowledge doubles every two years; clinical knowledge doubles every 18 months; and average human knowledge doubles every 13 months. Looking to the very near future, experts say that "the internet of things" will lead to the doubling of knowledge every 12 hours![5] We have clearly entered the era of an increase in knowledge.

During the same time we are witnessing an increase in all of those categories of natural knowledge, there is also a tremendous increase in the understanding of end-times prophecy as Bible students "run to and fro" within the Scriptures to see how Bible prophecy is unfolding in our day. More is known and understood about Bible prophecy today than at any other time in history. Progressive illumination is occurring within the church, as prophesied in Scripture.

Mountain Ranges

It took Lewis and Clark more than a month to get through the Rocky Mountains using the shortest route they could find. Looking at the Rocky Mountains can be misleading. From a distance, they appear to be a single rangle of mountains. In reality, there are multiple ranges side by side, which means that in some places, the Rockies are 300 miles wide.

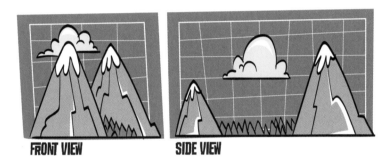

FRONT VIEW   SIDE VIEW

There are multiple mountain ranges and peaks in Bible prophecy as well. Just as we can see multiple peaks—separated by miles—in one view, some prophecies contain details that are separated by hundreds or even thousands of years. For example, many messianic prophecies (predictions about the coming Messiah) foresaw both a suffering servant and a conquering king. In classical Jewish thought, many believed there would be two Messiahs—one a conquering king, and the other a suffering servant who would be rejected by his people.

QUICK FACT: DID YOU KNOW...

that Isaiah 53 clearly portrays a Savior who suffers for the sins of others? Many details specific to the crucifixion are explained hundreds of years before Jesus died on the cross.

Here's another example. In Luke chapter 4, Jesus entered a synagogue and stood up to read a passage from Isaiah. According to verses 18-19 he said, "The Spirit of the Lord is on me, because he has anointed me to proclaim good news to the poor. He has sent me to proclaim freedom for the prisoners and recovery of sight for the blind, to set the oppressed free, to proclaim the year of the Lord's favor." Then Jesus put the scroll away and said, in verse 21, "Today this scripture is fulfilled in your hearing." He was quoting Isaiah 61:1-2, but he left off the second half of verse 2, which reads, "To proclaim the year of the Lord's favor *and the day of vengeance of our God*, to comfort all who mourn."

To those who were listening to Jesus that day, it seemed these fulfillments would happen in the same time period. But now, in hindsight, we know that the year of the Lord's favor (the age of grace) came first. It was initiated at the Messiah's first coming, when he suffered and died for sin. But the day of vengeance (the tribulation period) won't take place until the last days and concerns his second coming, when he will return to judge the earth and reign as King.

As we'll see in the next chapter, there are other Bible passages that are like mountain ranges. There are other prophecies God has progressively revealed and illuminated to students of Scripture.

PART 3:

IMPORTANT SECTIONS AND CATEGORIES

CHAPTER 10

Daniel's Visions

While I was speaking and praying, confessing my sin and the sin of my people Israel and making my request to the Lᴏʀᴅ my God for his holy hill—while I was still in prayer, Gabriel, the man I had seen in the earlier vision, came to me in swift flight about the time of the evening sacrifice. He instructed me and said to me, "Daniel, I have now come to give you insight and understanding."

DANIEL 9:20-22

In college, my drawing instructors always taught that in order to produce good art, we students needed to "bring up" the whole drawing together. Unless it is an intentional stylistic choice, a well-trained artist won't pick only one spot on the paper and immediately begin drawing fine details before moving to other areas to render.

Artists are taught to build the framework of a composition first, beginning with broad strokes and loose gestures while using their entire arm as they rough out a full sketch. An artist has to think about composition, positive and negative space, proportions, line of action, and other considerations as they work and rework their art loosely at first.

Once artists have adequately addressed those foundational considerations, they can confidently commit to a clean sketch using bold defining strokes that clearly frame the composition. Finally, once that key framework is committed to paper, they can continue bringing up the whole piece by adding shading and highlights, and finally by adding fine details using the smaller more coordinated muscles of the hand and fingers.

Studying prophecy is much the same. Students of Bible prophecy need to begin by familiarizing themselves with the entire Bible. Old Testament books like Daniel and Ezekiel lay down large foundational strokes of key information. Then other Old Testament books, like the books of the minor prophets and passages in Psalms, add more key details.

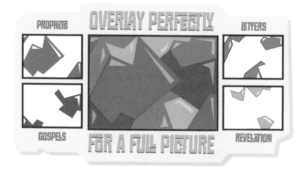

Then the Gospels and letters of the New Testament shine a bright light on many mysterious details that were veiled in the Old Testament. What the Old Testament concealed, the New Testament reveals. Mysteries like the rapture and the gap between the first and second comings of Christ, for example, were not made clearly known until the New Testament writings. Finally, the book of Revelation rounds out our prophetic understanding, effectively tying together every key theme in the Bible in stark detail. We'll work our way through all of these key passages in the next four chapters, beginning with the book of Daniel.

The Book of Daniel

The book of Daniel is the "Revelation" of the Old Testament. It sets the stage for the language and symbolism used later in Revelation. We'll discover in this chapter that Daniel provides the main framework that all other scriptural end-time passages fit into. Most are familiar with the narrative sections of Daniel—the lions' den, the fiery furnace, the handwriting on the wall, etc. Those are some incredible historical sections with relevant applications for us today, giving us insight and encouragement on how to live for the Lord faithfully in an increasingly pagan culture.

Alongside the wonderful narrative sections of Daniel we find a number of prophecies. Of the 12 chapters in Daniel, eight of them concern prophecy—a full two-thirds of the book. Written around 537 BC, the book of Daniel accurately details the four successive kingdoms from the Babylonian Empire to the Roman Empire, and provides a clear description of Western Europe during "the time of the end." Review the chart below showing an outline of Daniel, which will help you get a basic overview of the book.

OUTLINE OF THE BOOK OF DANIEL

CH 1 Daniel in captivity; refuses meat

CH 2 *Nebuchadnezzar's dream of a statue; Daniel's interpretation

CH 3 image of gold and the fiery furnace

CH 4 Nebuchadnezzar's dream of the tree and Daniel's interpretation

CH 5 a new king (Belshazzar) and a hand writing on the wall

CH 6 another new king (Cyrus) and Daniel in the lions' den

CH 7 *Daniel has a dream of 4 beasts that matches the statue vision of the kingdoms

CH 8 *Daniel has a vision of a ram and a goat (Greece vs. Medo-Persia)

CH 9 *Daniel is visited by an angel and receives the prophecy of the 70 "weeks"

CH 10 Daniel's vision of a mysterious messenger

CH 11 *more about Greece, a prototype of the antichrist, and end-time events

CH 12 *the messenger reveals more details of the future tribulation period

*CONTAINS END-TIMES PROPHECY

The first six chapters tell the historical account of Daniel living as a captive in Babylon from his teenage years into his old age. These six chapters span 70 years and three different rulers of Babylon. Within the first section, Daniel interprets two of Nebuchadnezzar's dreams containing detailed prophecies. The second section of Daniel (7–12) consists of various prophecies given directly to Daniel through dreams, visions, and direct communication with angels.

QUICK FACT: DID YOU KNOW...

that in the Bible, the term *angel* simply means "messenger"? In several places in the Old Testament, the being called "the angel of the LORD" was most likely the pre-incarnate Jesus. In Daniel chapter 3, Jesus was likely the fourth man in the fiery furnace who looked like a "son of God." When Jesus shows up in the Old Testament, it's known as a *Christophany*.

Certain sections of Daniel are not written chronologically. Instead, the book is organized into sections that relate to Israel and sections that relate to Gentile nations. Interestingly, chapter 1 is written in Hebrew, chapters 2–7 are written in Aramaic—the Gentile language of the day—and chapters 8–12 switch back to Hebrew. The language used in each section is directly related to the people group impacted by the prophecies contained in those chapters.

The concept of the prophetic mountain peaks, described in the previous chapter of this book, come into play with certain prophecies found in Daniel. In several places we find prophecies about world events being described, then in the next phrase or sentence Daniel abruptly switches his focus to end-time events.

Space does not allow for a full explanation of the book of Daniel, but I'd like to draw your attention to a few important themes that are relevant to end-times prophecy and help lay the foundation for the chapters that follow.

Three Key Prophetic Themes
The Succession of Kingdoms

In chapter 2 of this book, I cited Nebuchadnezzar's vision of world empires (Daniel chapter 2) as evidence for the divine authorship of the Bible. This major 2,600-year-old prophecy predicting the succession of world empires and the time of the end is so grand in scope and so accurate in its description that Bible critics either have to ignore it or invent weak arguments in their attempts to explain away its accuracy or date of origin.

The successive kingdoms of Babylon, Medo-Persia, Greece, and Rome, followed by the Roman Empire splitting into two legs (fulfilled in AD 395 when the Eastern leg separated from Rome and established its capital in Constantinople, which is modern-day Istanbul), then breaking into individual nation-states, is an accurate description of history.

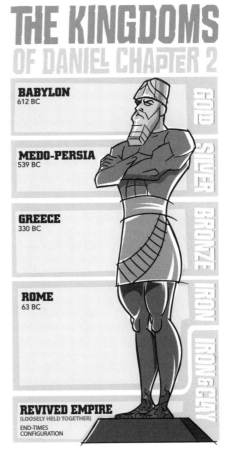

THE KINGDOMS
OF DANIEL CHAPTER 2

BABYLON
612 BC

MEDO-PERSIA
539 BC

GREECE
330 BC

ROME
63 BC

REVIVED EMPIRE
(LOOSELY HELD TOGETHER)
END-TIMES
CONFIGURATION

GOLD SILVER BRONZE IRON IRON & CLAY

Daniel then shows us that the final configuration of the area ruled by the Roman Empire in the last days—the feet and toes—will be struck by a rock that completely destroys the statue. Then, according to the vision, the rock will become a mountain and fill the whole earth.

Prophecy experts take this to mean that a revived but unstable Roman Empire of sorts will be in place before or at least by the early part of the tribulation period, and that this empire will be utterly destroyed when Christ returns to set up his millennial kingdom. We are given this interpretation in Daniel 2:44-45: "In the time of those kings, the God of heaven will set up a kingdom that will never be destroyed, nor will it be left to another people. It will crush all those kingdoms and bring them to an end, but it will itself endure forever. This is the meaning of the vision of the rock cut out of a mountain, but not by human hands—a rock that broke the iron, the bronze, the clay, the silver and the gold to pieces. The great God has shown the king what will take place in the future. The dream is true and its interpretation is trustworthy."

Most prophecy experts see the current European Union as the foundation for— if not the actual—end-times configuration of the statue's feet. They see the ten toes as ten elite rulers (of nations or world regions) who will rule for a short time with the antichrist. The ten horns described in Revelation 17:12 support this idea by the interpretation given there. It states that they are ten rulers.

The Introduction of the Antichrist

The book of Daniel provides the most complete picture of the antichrist found in the Old Testament. I use this pop-culture term, antichrist, because it is familiar to most, although this term is not found in the book of Daniel, nor in the book of Revelation. The evil end-time ruler is referred to as the antichrist only in the books of 1 and 2 John. In chapter 4 of this book, we learned about this individual and listed several of his titles found in Scripture, but antichrist seems to have become the term that encapsulates all of them.

> 1 John 2:18—Dear children, this is the last hour; and as you have heard that the antichrist is coming, even now many antichrists have come. This is how we know it is the last hour.

There are several references to this evil end-time world ruler in the book of Daniel, beginning in chapter 7. Verse 8 refers to the antichrist as "the little horn" and gives us some details about his rise to power and other characteristics. When Daniel asked for the meaning of the prophecy, he was given the following information about the antichrist in verse 25: "He will speak against the Most High and oppress his holy people and try to change the set times and the laws. The holy people will be delivered into his hands for a time, times and half a time."

Then chapter 8 provides more details about the evil end-times ruler. We read this in verses 23-25: "In the latter part of their reign, when rebels have become completely wicked, a fierce-looking king, a master of intrigue, will arise. He will become very strong, but not by his own power. He will cause astounding devastation and will succeed in whatever he does. He will destroy those who are mighty, the holy people. He will cause deceit to prosper, and he will consider himself superior. When they feel secure, he will destroy many and take his stand against the Prince of princes. Yet he will be destroyed, but not by human power."

We also find in Daniel 9 that the antichrist will come from the people who will destroy the temple after the death of the Messiah (this destruction was carried out by Rome in AD 70). He will also confirm or enforce a seven-year covenant with Israel and many, which he will break in the middle of the covenant.

Finally, in Daniel 11:36-39 we read, "The king will do as he pleases. He will exalt and magnify himself above every god and will say unheard-of things against the God of gods. He will be successful until the time of wrath is completed, for what has been determined must take place. He will show no regard for the gods of his ancestors or for the one desired by women, nor will he regard any god, but will exalt himself above them all. Instead of them, he will honor a god of fortresses; a god unknown to his ancestors he will honor with gold and silver, with precious stones and costly gifts. He will attack the mightiest fortresses with the help of a foreign god and will greatly honor those who acknowledge him. He will make them rulers over many people and will distribute the land at a price."

So, the initial puzzle pieces we gather from the book of Daniel concerning the antichrist are many, and when we compare those sections, we can paint a fairly clear picture of this individual.

The Seventy "Weeks"

The third key prophetic theme found in Daniel is the 70 weeks (of years) in chapter 9.

This chapter, particularly the last four verses, is absolutely critical to understanding end-times theology. There is so much packed into those four verses that it's like picking up a tennis ball and discovering that it weighs as much as a cannonball. If you don't study anything else in this chapter, I would encourage you to spend time getting a grip on this section. Let's begin by reading Daniel 9:24-27, and I would encourage you to read through the passage a few times before continuing to the commentary below.

Seventy "sevens" are decreed for your people and your holy city to finish transgression, to put an end to sin, to atone for wickedness, to bring in everlasting righteousness, to seal up vision and prophecy and to anoint the Most Holy Place.

Know and understand this: From the time the word goes out to restore and rebuild Jerusalem until the Anointed One, the ruler, comes, there will be seven "sevens," and sixty-two "sevens." It will be rebuilt with streets and a trench, but in times of trouble. After the sixty-two "sevens," the Anointed One will be put to death and will have nothing. The people of the ruler who will come will destroy the city and the sanctuary. The end will come like a flood: War will continue until the end, and desolations have been decreed. He will confirm a covenant with many for one "seven." In the middle of the "seven" he will put an end to sacrifice and offering. And at the temple he will set up an abomination that causes desolation, until the end that is decreed is poured out on him.

At the beginning of Daniel 9, we find Daniel studying Bible prophecy. Based on the prophecies of Jeremiah, Daniel understood that the Jewish captivity in Babylon was to last 70 years. Once again, we find Daniel fasted and prayed. As he prayed, Gabriel, the messenger angel, showed up with an incredibly long-ranging prophecy. Daniel had inquired about the end of the Jewish exile, and in response, God sent a prophecy that covered all of Jewish history!

The context of Daniel praying about the 70 years of captivity gives us the first hint that the 70 "sevens" refers to "sevens of years." In other words, 70 sets of seven years. The accuracy of those years in the fulfillment of prophecy—which we will look at below—confirms this is exactly what was meant by the angel Gabriel. So the full time frame in view here is 490 years (using the Jewish 360-day lunar calendar in place at the time this prophecy was given).

The Full Scope of Jewish History

The foundational statement in this prophecy gives us the full scope of Jewish history. Notice that the 70 "sevens" were decreed, or inexorably planned, for Daniel's people and holy city. In other words, this prophecy was fixed, exact, and unchangeable. Daniel was Jewish. The holy city of the Jewish people was and is Jerusalem. This prophecy was specifically for the Jewish people.

The Timing of the Messiah's Arrival Foretold

This amazing prophecy also provided the exact time frame for the arrival of Jesus's first coming. It foretold that there will be 69 sets of seven years, or 483 years on the Jewish calendar, between a call to rebuild Jerusalem and the arrival of the Anointed One.

We know from Nehemiah 2:1 that in 445 BC, King Artaxerxes allowed Nehemiah to go and rebuild Jerusalem (beginning with the walls around the city). Nehemiah 1 tells us this happened in the month of Nisan in the twentieth year of Artaxerxes. Long story short, we can identify this exact date based on historical and archeological records. Fast-forward 483 years and we come to the spring of AD 31, the time of Jesus's triumphal entry on Palm Sunday.

Many credible prophecy experts have taken the time to calculate all the dates and study the historical references that back up the specific year identified in Nehemiah 2, and they make an extremely strong case that this prophecy of 483 Jewish years was fulfilled to the exact day!

Messiah's Death Prophesied

After the 62 "sevens," the Anointed One would be put to death and "have nothing." This was clearly fulfilled at the cross, where Jesus died. He literally owned nothing and had to be buried in a borrowed tomb. All seemed lost—at least until the resurrection!

The AD 70 Destruction of Jerusalem and the Temple Prophesied

The people of "the ruler who will come" will destroy the city and the sanctuary. This is the first clear prophecy about the destruction of Jerusalem and the temple. This occurred in AD 70 at the hand of the Roman military leader Titus, who would later become emperor.

The Tribulation Period Prophesied

We find another mountain-peak prophecy in Daniel 9 with a mysterious gap taking place between verses 26 and 27. This gap is where the church age fits in. Notice that in the sequence of the prophecy, we are told that the sanctuary—the temple—will be destroyed. Then, in the very next verse, we read that the antichrist will defile an already-standing temple. We go from the destruction of one temple in Jerusalem to the presence of another temple that will be defiled by the antichrist. Logic demands there is a gap of time between the two verses—a gap during which the temple mentioned in verse 27 will be built. We also learn here that the antichrist figure will "confirm a covenant" for the final set of seven years of this prophecy, and that he will break the covenant in the middle of that seven years.

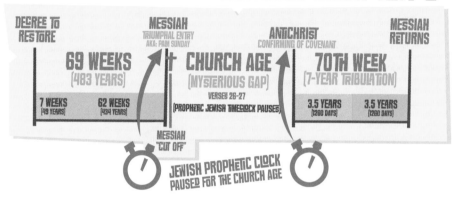

The mysterious gap between the Messiah's being "cut off" and the beginning of the last set of seven years—the tribulation period—is where we are now. It is a period during which God's plan of salvation is made known to the entire world—the Gentile nations. But when the final seven years of human history begins with the confirmation of the covenant, the final seven years of this prophecy will also begin.

I believe the Jewish time-clock for the first 483 years most likely paused at the triumphal entry of Jesus, which took place on what is commonly referred to as Palm Sunday. This time-clock will resume the moment the pen is lifted at the signing of a peace treaty between Israel and other nations.

Now that we've seen how Daniel provides the key framework for end-time events, let's look at another key prophetic section of Scripture—one in which Jesus himself provides a lot more details about the last days. This passage is known as the Olivet Discourse.

CHAPTER 11

The Olivet Discourse

Jesus left the temple and was walking away when his disciples came up to him to call his attention to its buildings. "Do you see all these things?" he asked. "Truly I tell you, not one stone here will be left on another; every one will be thrown down." As Jesus was sitting on the Mount of Olives, the disciples came to him privately. "Tell us," they said, "when will this happen, and what will be the sign of your coming and of the end of the age?"

MATTHEW 24:1-3

I was working in Washington, DC, just 2.3 miles from the Pentagon when it was hit by a plane hijacked by Islamic terrorists on the morning of September 11, 2001. With everyone trying to leave the city, the chaos became like nothing I had ever seen. Plumes of smoke rose from the Pentagon just across the Potomac River. Jets flew overhead. Firetruck and police sirens blared from every direction. There was absolute gridlock on every street. Frantic pedestrians and frustrated drivers were gripped with a current of fear as word spread that another plane may be heading for the White House or the US Capitol building.

This was a game-changer. The mainland attacks on the Pentagon and the World Trade Center were unprecedented in American history. These massive buildings were the symbols of the military and financial strength of the world's greatest superpower. Prior to 8:46 a.m., when the first tower was hit, and 9:37 a.m., when the Pentagon was hit, both symbols of strength seemed as secure and untouchable as anything on earth could be. But this wasn't the first time that well-known symbols of seemingly untouchable strength and favor were destroyed.

Beginning in 19 BC, King Herod I began a massive construction campaign to enlarge and beautify the Jewish temple and surrounding area in Jerusalem. The main project of Herod's rebuilding effort was completed before he died in 4 BC, but the work continued for more than 60 years after his death. It was finally completed in AD 63. The finished Temple Mount plaza was so large it could have held 29 NFL football fields. This massive complex of buildings sat on the highest point of the city. Constructed from large, white hewn stones with sections of the temple overlaid with gold, the structures' magnificence glistened in the bright mid-Eastern sun and could be seen for miles. The temple especially was truly the glory of Jerusalem.

1ST TEMPLE
DESTROYED 587 BC

2ND TEMPLE
"HEROD'S TEMPLE"
DESTROYED AD 70

The disciples—having seen Jesus perform miracles, enter Jerusalem while being hailed as king, unleash a holy temper-tantrum in the temple courts, and defy the religious leaders in front of the crowds—began to sense that it was about to "get real" in terms of the coming kingdom. They knew a significant change had occurred in Jesus's earthly ministry. The lowly and humble countercultural teacher was now entering a new phase of ministry during which his kingdom authority began to be revealed. They did not understand the cross, the resurrection, or the long church age yet, but they sensed a transition was taking place.

With all that fresh on their minds, as they walked from the massive temple complex and the many support buildings, the disciples commented on the beauty of it all. Then Jesus dropped a bomb. He told them it would all be destroyed. Leveled. Not one single stone left on top of another. His sobering comments struck hard, so as soon as they had Jesus alone, they asked him about the details of the destruction of the temple, of his return, and of the end of the world. In their minds, all these events were closely related.

Jesus could have said, "No comment," or he could have given them a vague answer. But he didn't dodge the questions, nor did he chastise them for asking. He approved of their questions and in fact gave a rather long response.

This conversation between Jesus and his disciples is known as the Olivet Discourse, which is a fancy and more concise way of saying "the talk Jesus had with his disciples on the Mount of Olives next to the temple area." Aside from the book of Revelation, it contains the longest passage about end-times prophecy in the New Testament. It is also the second-longest continuous teaching of Jesus. The longest uninterrupted instruction we have from him is the Sermon on the Mount.

The importance of the timing of Jesus's instruction cannot be overstated. This message came right after he was rejected by his people—as represented by the Jewish religious leaders—and just before the events leading to his crucifixion.

Jesus's response to the disciples provides a clear outline of end-time events and fits perfectly into the framework of Daniel as studied in the last chapter. The prophecies in Daniel provide a broad overview of world empires and Jewish history leading to the time of the end. The Olivet Discourse provides a closer view of church-age events leading up to and during the tribulation period itself.

If I could use an analogy from the world of cinema, Daniel offers us a wide establishing shot of the forest, while Jesus provides a tighter medium shot of the end-time trees in the Olivet Discourse. Then the book of Revelation—which we will study in the next chapter—provides a close-up shot of the seven-year tribulation period, the millennial kingdom, and the final eternal state.

The Olivet Discourse is found in Matthew 24–25, Mark 13, and Luke 21:5-36. No single passage contains every word of Jesus's teaching in the discourse, and each writer focused on different details with their particular audience in mind. A careful comparison of all three accounts provides a more complete view, and the account in Matthew provides the longest version of the teaching.

All of what Jesus spoke of in the discourse was future prophecy. His prophecy about every stone being torn down was fulfilled in exact detail 34 years after the prophecy was given. Literally every single stone of the temple building was thrown down so that the Romans could access all the gold that had melted between the cracks when the temple had been burned down during the attack on Jerusalem. You can still see many of the large stones lying at the base of the Temple Mount today. We know the rest of Jesus's prophecies will be fulfilled in exact detail as well.

The Disciples' Questions

The disciples asked Jesus two questions, but one had two parts—so they essentially asked three questions. In their minds, the questions were closely related.

When all three Gospel accounts are compared, here is the essence of the three questions:

1. What is the sign that Jerusalem and the temple are about to be destroyed?
2. What is the sign of your return at the very end?
3. What is the sign that this age is coming to a close?

In Western culture, we like well-organized presentations given in chronological order. In ancient Jewish culture, however, that wasn't always done. We saw in the previous chapter how Daniel organized his writing based on the audience he was writing to. Similarly, the Gospel writers structured their accounts to suit the primary audience they were addressing. For example, Luke wrote primarily for Gentiles, whereas Matthew's audience was primarily Jewish. In movies, we are used to nonlinear story lines that include flashback scenes and foreshadows of coming events. Well, in the case of the Olivet Discourse, Jesus answered the disciples' questions out of order. He answered the last question first, the first question second, and the second question last.

Let's start by looking at Matthew 24:4-6: "Watch out that no one deceives you. For *many will come in my name, claiming, 'I am the Messiah,' and will deceive many.* You will hear of *wars and rumors of wars*, but see to it that you are not alarmed. Such things must happen, *but the end is still to come*" (emphasis mine). (See also Mark 13:6-7 and Luke 21:8-9.)

Before answering any of the questions, Jesus provided some key details about the general characteristics of the church age. In essence, he listed several "nonsigns" that his followers would observe throughout the age. There would be false messiahs, threats of war, and many regional wars. That is exactly what we have seen happen as the church age has unfolded. But Jesus said these would not be the signs of the end. He said these things must occur, "but the end is still to come." Then he shifted gears and answered the disciples' third question first.

Answer to the third question first: What is the sign that this current era (the church age) is coming to a close?

Matthew 24:7-8—"Nation will rise against nation, and kingdom against kingdom. There will be **famines** *and* **earthquakes** *in various places. All these are the beginning of birth pains"* (emphasis mine). (See also Mark 13:8 and Luke 21:10-11.)

After giving a list of nonsigns, Jesus revealed clear, specific signs that would indicate when the church age was winding down. The phrase "nation against nation, and kingdom against kingdom" was a Jewish idiom of that time period meaning *world war*—massive, worldwide military conflict. Jesus was saying that regional wars would be common fare throughout church history, but when you see the whole world at war, that would be a key sign marking the beginning of the birth pains that would bring about the end.

Following this, the birth pains would continue. When a woman is in labor, the birth pains gradually increase in frequency and severity. Likewise, we should expect to see the end-time birth pains increase in number and severity following a world war. Can we point to a time in church history marked by a world war followed by increasing famine, earthquakes, and (Luke adds) pestilence or disease? Absolutely.

World War I involved 32 countries and resulted in 18 million deaths. It lasted from 1914–1918 and was immediately followed by massive European famine and the 1918 Flu Pandemic, which killed another 50-100 million people. A short 21 years separated WWI and WWII, and the latter saw 50-80 million people killed. It was, in essence, a continuation of WWI, with the same general players on each side.

QUICK FACT: DID YOU KNOW...

that WWI introduced chemical weapons and WWII introduced nuclear weapons to the world?

We'll cover earthquakes in a later chapter, but let's just say there is clear empirical evidence that earthquakes have increased in frequency and severity since this time period as well. Prophecy expert Dr. Tim LaHaye pointed out in his book *Are We Living in the End Times?* the following facts:

...during the period from 2000 to 2008, the total number of earth-quakes worldwide each year that were recorded with a magnitude of 3.0 to 3.9 increased from 4,827 to an astonishing 11,735. Like-wise, those with a magnitude of 4.0 to 4.9 increased in number from 8,008 in the year 2000 to 12,291 in 2008 while those measuring 5.0 to 5.9 rose from 1,344 to 1,768.

LaHaye went on to describe how the number of earthquakes worldwide has risen so dramatically that in 2009 the USGS National Earthquake Informa-tion Center stopped keeping track of earthquakes that were smaller than 4.5 in magnitude unless damage or loss of life demanded it. This trend has contin-ued with record-breaking earthquake swarms taking place in 2017. Likewise, we have seen famine and disease continue to grip the world (more on the signs of nature in chapter 15).

Interestingly, World War I helped the Zionist movement and set the stage for the Jewish people to return to their homeland, and World War II led to Israel's official rebirth as a nation, as prophesied in Scripture. Is it a coincidence that the end-time sign Jesus said would mark the beginning of the end also led to the prophetic fulfillment of Israel becoming a nation again? I think not. Many Old Testament prophecies about Israel's restoration tell us this momentous event will occur in the last days. So, we say with confidence that WWI was *the* sign that we were beginning to transition into the last days.

The answer to the first question second: What is the sign that Jerusalem and the temple are about to be destroyed?

Luke 21:20-24—"*When you see Jerusalem being surrounded by armies*, you will know that its desolation is near. Then let those who are in Judea *flee to the moun-tains*, let those in the city get out, and let those in the country not enter the city. For this is the time of punishment in fulfillment of all that has been written. How dreadful it will be in those days for pregnant women and nursing moth-ers! There will be great distress in the land and *wrath against this people*. They will fall by the sword and will be taken as prisoners to all the nations. *Jerusa-lem will be trampled on by the Gentiles until the times of the Gentiles are fulfilled*" (emphasis mine).

Matthew 24:15-21—"So when you see standing in the holy place '*the abomina-tion that causes desolation*,' spoken of through the prophet Daniel—let the reader understand—then *let those who are in Judea flee to the mountains.* Let no one on the housetop go down to take anything out of the house. Let no one in the field go back to get their cloak. How dreadful it will be in those days for pregnant women and nursing mothers! Pray that your flight will not take place in winter or on the Sabbath. For then *there will be great distress, unequaled from the beginning of the world until now*—and never to be equaled again" (emphasis mine).

There are distinct and important differences in the Matthew and Luke accounts, including their chronology. When it comes to Bible prophecy, one event can foreshadow a similar yet fuller future prophetic event. Some experts believe these two passages are describing the same event, while others, such as Chuck Missler and Arnold Fruchtenbaum, point out the subtle but important differences.

I'm not dogmatic about this, but I tend to agree with Missler and Fruchtenbaum that Luke and Matthew describe two different but similar events—one being the destruction of Jerusalem in AD 70, and the other being the desecration of the future temple at the midpoint of the tribulation.

As for the first event, early Jewish Christians in Jerusalem took Jesus's prophecy seriously. The Jewish historian Flavius Josephus recorded—in his work *The Wars of the Jews*—that during the destruction of the city in AD 70, an estimated 1.1 million Jewish people were killed, and roughly 100,000 were taken captive. The Greek historian Eusebius Pamphili recorded that Christians, however, fled Jerusalem when they had a brief opportunity to do so after seeing Jerusalem surrounded by the Romans. Eusebius said that Christians fled to an area called Pella (in modern-day Jordan) before the destruction of Jerusalem.

In a similar fashion, the Matthew account instructs Jewish people in the future tribulation period to flee Jerusalem when they see the abomination of desolation take place. This future landmark event was foreshadowed by Antiochus Epiphanes in the second century BC, and is clearly detailed in Daniel, the Olivet Discourse, and in Revelation. The abomination of desolation will occur at the exact midpoint of the tribulation and will begin the great tribulation, also known as the time of Jacob's trouble.

This is when the gloves will come off, the antichrist will break the seven-year covenant with Israel, and like a super-Hitler, he will attempt to annihilate the Jewish people. Sadly, we are told he will have great success in this evil campaign, yet a remnant of Jewish people will manage to survive and will turn to Jesus just before his return.

When this critical turning point takes place, the Jewish people—like their Christian counterparts in AD 70—are told to flee Jerusalem. Apparently the antichrist's evil persecution will not ramp up gradually, but will commence with full force immediately after the abomination of desolation event. We don't know all the details of this event, but it will clearly defile the rebuilt temple and it will be offensive beyond compare.

So, Luke described events that would occur *before* the sign of the end of the age (WWI, etc.), but Matthew described events that would occur *after* the sign of the end of the age. We know this by his all-important use of the word "then" in Matthew 24:9. *After* the sign of the end of the age, *then* tribulation-period events will occur. It's important to keep in mind that *similar* does not mean the *same*. It's equally important to remember that every single nuance of Scripture is intentional and meaningful.

Matthew 5:18—For assuredly, I say to you, till heaven and earth pass away, one jot or one tittle will by no means pass from the law till all is fulfilled (NKJV).

QUICK FACT: DID YOU KNOW...

that the jot and the tittle are the tiniest strokes made when writing in Hebrew? The jot looks like an apostrophe and the tittle is just a miniscule letter extension that helps differentiate certain Hebrew letters.

Answer to the second question last: What is the sign of your return at the very end?

Matthew 24:29-30—"*Immediately after* the distress of those days the *sun will be darkened*, and the *moon* will not give its light; the *stars will fall* from the sky, and the heavenly bodies will be shaken. *Then will appear the sign of the Son of Man* in heaven. And then all the peoples of the earth will mourn when they *see the Son of Man coming on the clouds of heaven*, with power and *great glory*" (emphasis mine). (See also Mark 13:14-23.)

Finally, Jesus answered the disciples' second question: "What is the sign of your return at the very end?" In Matthew 24:9-26 Jesus detailed events of the first and second halves of the tribulation period that line up perfectly with the book of Revelation and the initial end-times prophecies in the book of Daniel.

We are told in all three accounts of the Olivet Discourse that just before the actual event of Christ's return, there will be a complete blackout. The sun, moon, and stars will go dark. Scripture then tells us the sign of the Lord will appear. We don't know what this sign will be, but it will occur just before the Son of Man is seen "coming on the clouds of heaven with power and great glory."

We know from Revelation that at his return, Jesus will be riding a white war horse followed by the armies of heaven—including you and me (if you know Christ as Savior before the rapture) and millions of angels—to defeat the antichrist and his armies in Jerusalem. Perhaps the sign is the brightness of the glory of Christ as the heavenly dimension suddenly breaks in on the total darkness.

What a remarkable day that will be!

CHAPTER 12

John's Revelation

The revelation from Jesus Christ, which God gave him to show his servants what must soon take place. He made it known by sending his angel to his servant John.

REVELATION 1:1

As I mentioned in chapter 9, I went to a Christian summer camp as a kid. I was 12 years old and wasn't a Christian at the time. I knew almost nothing about Jesus or what it really meant to be a Christian. My family had heard about the camp from friends who had gone the year before. They told us about the fun they had hiking and water-skiing. So, we went.

The activities were a blast, but the main purpose of the camp was to introduce children to Jesus Christ. We had daily Bible lessons and our counselors led devotions and prayed with us each night. On the last day of camp there was an event called "Hike Through the Bible," during which we would hike to various locations around the camp and see performances that brought different Bible stories to life. Camp counselors acted out key Bible characters and events from Genesis to Revelation.

The only scene I really remember in detail is one of the last, which showed Satan being bound for 1,000 years. For some reason the angry camp counselor with a shredded T-shirt, chains on his arms, and black makeup on his eyes stuck in my memory.

That camp was my introduction to Christianity and the book of Revelation. My full knowledge of Christianity by the time I left the camp was that Christians liked to sing about a guy named Abraham, who apparently had many sons; they believed Jesus died for our sins; and they believed that some really crazy stuff would happen at the end of this age. It was the first time I learned that the Bible claimed to tell us how the world would end, and it was the first time I ever heard of the book of Revelation.

Essential Background Information

When it comes to Revelation, you may feel a bit bewildered like I did at camp. Or, perhaps you have already had some exposure to the book, but you still feel that it is complex and beyond understanding. I hope this chapter will help change that.

Revelation was written by the apostle John, who was known as "the disciple whom [Jesus] loved" (John 19:26). John had an especially close relationship with Jesus during his earthly ministry. He was the sole disciple who did not abandon the Lord during the events of the crucifixion, and he was the only one who (at least according to church tradition) did not die a martyr's death. He was, however, exiled to the island of Patmos by the Romans. That is where he received the visions that are recorded in Revelation. John also wrote four other New Testament books.

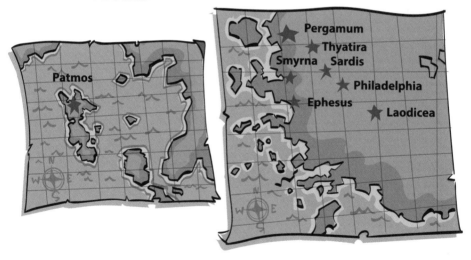

The Surprisingly Simple Structure of Revelation

Many people I talk with seem to think Revelation is too complex to understand, or that it is irrelevant, divisive, or just plain confusing. People are often surprised to learn that Revelation is the only book of the Bible that promises a blessing to those who read it. It's also the primary source of information regarding the details about Satan's ultimate defeat and our ultimate victory. It's no wonder that the enemy does his best to discourage God's people from reading this amazing book.

Revelation 1:3—Blessed is the one who reads aloud the words of this prophecy, and blessed are those who hear it and take to heart what is written in it, because the time is near.

A friend of mine recounted a time when he felt led to read the entire book of Revelation in one sitting during an airplane flight. He was overwhelmed with tears as he read it—he sensed that God was impressing upon on his heart, "This is my love letter to you." Revelation is exactly that. Our loving heavenly Father wants his children to be informed about what is going to take place. He also wants to warn the world of the coming judgment so people have the opportunity to turn to him and avoid judgment.

John 3:17—For God did not send his Son into the world to condemn the world, but to save the world through him.

Revelation is one of the more simply structured books in the Bible. We are provided with the outline of the book in the first chapter:

Revelation 1:19—Write, therefore, what you have seen, what is now and what will take place later.

1. Things You Have Seen (Glorified Christ in Heaven, 1:12-18)

2. Things Which Are (Direction to the Seven Churches, chapters 2–3)

3. Things That Take Place After (Future/Tribulation/Kingdom/ Eternity, chapters 4–22)

Boom. There's your outline for the book of Revelation.

There are also specific phrases throughout Revelation demonstrating that it is written primarily in chronological order. Phrases like "after this," "when he had opened the seventh seal," "the seven last plagues," and "after these things." These are time-oriented sequential phrases and there is a natural progression and buildup of events throughout the book. We even find that the seal, trumpet, and bowl judgments are each numbered in order, from one through seven.

The main section that is not in chronological order is chapters 10–14. These are parenthetical—or overview—chapters. They provide more context for some of the broad themes and extended events of the tribulation period. It's almost as if they serve like an intermission in the middle of the book. After describing the seal and trumpet judgments, John paused to provide more context and detail, and to let you catch your breath. Then he resumed the chronological order in chapter 15 with the bowl judgments. Take a look at this simplified outline of the book, then let's take a slightly deeper dive and look at a more detailed outline.

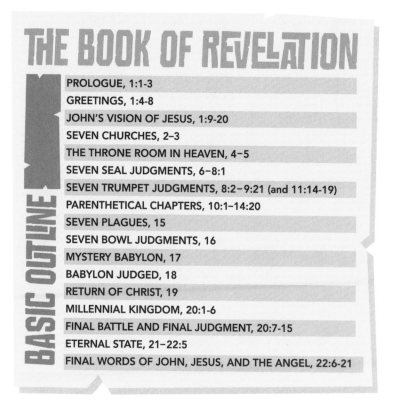

THE BOOK OF REVELATION

BASIC OUTLINE

PROLOGUE, 1:1-3

GREETINGS, 1:4-8

JOHN'S VISION OF JESUS, 1:9-20

SEVEN CHURCHES, 2–3

THE THRONE ROOM IN HEAVEN, 4–5

SEVEN SEAL JUDGMENTS, 6–8:1

SEVEN TRUMPET JUDGMENTS, 8:2–9:21 (and 11:14-19)

PARENTHETICAL CHAPTERS, 10:1–14:20

SEVEN PLAGUES, 15

SEVEN BOWL JUDGMENTS, 16

MYSTERY BABYLON, 17

BABYLON JUDGED, 18

RETURN OF CHRIST, 19

MILLENNIAL KINGDOM, 20:1-6

FINAL BATTLE AND FINAL JUDGMENT, 20:7-15

ETERNAL STATE, 21–22:5

FINAL WORDS OF JOHN, JESUS, AND THE ANGEL, 22:6-21

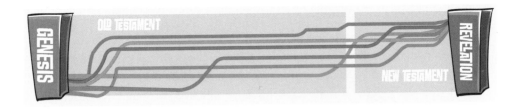

Placement of the Seal, Trumpet, and Bowl Judgments

My loosely held view is that the seal and trumpet judgments all occur before the midpoint of the tribulation period, and the bowl judgments occur during the second half. But I should mention that there are many good Bible prophecy teachers and friends who differ on their views about the timing of the various judgments.

There are three main views (with additional slight variations of each). The chronology is the same (sequential), but the timing of the various judgments fall differently into the three sections of the tribulation. Those three sections being (1) the gap period (in between the rapture and the signing of the peace treaty, which will begin the tribulation); (2) the first 3.5 years; and (3) the second 3.5 years.

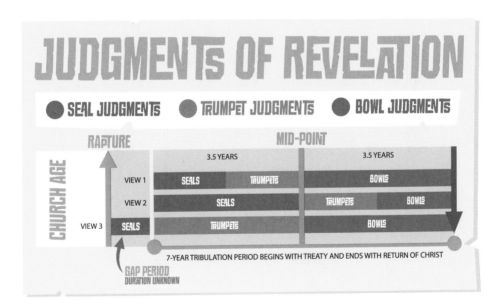

JUDGMENTS OF REVELATION

● SEAL JUDGMENTS   ● TRUMPET JUDGMENTS   ● BOWL JUDGMENTS

RAPTURE   MID-POINT

CHURCH AGE

	3.5 YEARS		3.5 YEARS	
VIEW 1	SEALS	TRUMPETS	BOWLS	
VIEW 2	SEALS		TRUMPETS	BOWLS
VIEW 3	SEALS	TRUMPETS	BOWLS	

7-YEAR TRIBULATION PERIOD BEGINS WITH TREATY AND ENDS WITH RETURN OF CHRIST

GAP PERIOD
DURATION UNKNOWN

A More Detailed Outline of Revelation

Because the bulk of Revelation (chapters 4–19) deals with the events of the tribulation period, it is helpful to get an overview of the key events that will occur in this time frame. Now that you've seen the simplified outline and the charts depicting the judgments, consider this more detailed chronological order of the book:

Introduction and Churches (Revelation 1–3)

- John sees glorified Christ
- Jesus's direction to the seven churches

Throne Room (Revelation 4–5)

John is caught up to heaven's throne room (this designates the rapture, which ends the church era)

Jesus found worthy to open the title deed to the earth

Tribulation Period Begins (Revelation 6–7)

- Antichrist revealed when a treaty is confirmed between Israel and "many"
- 3.5-year ministry of the two witnesses begins (chapter 11)
- First seal—antichrist conquers with diplomacy and intrigue
- Antichrist becomes the head of ten-nation (or region) confederacy
- Antichrist establishes his capital (rebuilt Babylon or "Mystery" Babylon"*)
- Jewish temple rebuilt, sacrifices resume
- Second seal—war (**Gog-Magog War of Ezekiel 38–39, ***or Psalm 83 War, ****or some other war)
- Third seal—famine (result of war and/or supply control by elite leaders)
- Fourth seal—plague and disease
- Fifth seal—martyrdom

- Sixth seal—Global calamity (massive earthquakes, destructive meteor showers)
- 144,000 Jewish evangelists sealed/commissioned

The added word mystery *is important and hints that the location may be somewhere other than literal Babylon, which is in modern-day Iraq. Prophecy experts have made strong arguments for Mystery Babylon as being modern-day Rome, while others (more recently) suggest that it may be Mecca. Still others say there is both a religious and a political Babylon.*

**Possible placement for event for various reasons, but another strong possible placement is in the gap period prior to the beginning of the tribulation period.*

***I believe the Psalm 83 war has already occurred during one of (or all of) Israel's conventional wars since her rebirth in 1948. (War of Independence, Six-Day War, Yom Kippur War, etc.) Those wars involved the exact countries (bordering Israel on all sides), and had the same motivations as described in Psalm 83.*

****With the restraining influence of the church and the Holy Spirit out of the picture due to the rapture, mankind will quickly and demonically descend into further violence and unrestrained aggression leading to several wars described in Revelation. This may also be war caused by some countries resisting the antichrist's overreaching power grab.*

Judgments Escalate (Revelation 6–7)

- Seventh seal—silence in heaven because of what is about to happen
- Massive storms and a massive earthquake
- First trumpet—hail, fire, and blood burns one-third of the earth, one-third of the trees, and all of the world's grass (some experts believe this may indicate a coronal mass ejection from the sun)
- Second trumpet—mountain-sized meteor crashes into the sea, destroying life in one-third of it
- Third trumpet—a fiery meteor or a rogue star crashes on land and poisons the headwaters of major rivers, poisoning one-third of the water and causing many to die from drinking it
- Fourth trumpet—all celestial light dimmed by one-third (probably due to trumpets 1–3)

- Judgments escalate again as John sees an eagle announcing "three woes," referring to the last three trumpet judgments
- Fifth trumpet—another large meteor or star falls to earth, large enough to crack the earth's crust, which opens up "the Abyss" and releases a fallen angel named "Destroyer" and demonic locusts that will torture, for five months, those who refuse to accept Jesus as Savior
- Sixth trumpet—four Euphrates angels released who will lead 200 million demonic, fire-breathing horse creatures

Parenthetical Chapters (Revelation 10–14)

- Angel and the little scroll
- Ministry of two witnesses detailed
- Seventh trumpet
- Sign of the woman and the dragon
- Details about the beast of the sea (antichrist)
- Details about the beast of the earth (false prophet)
- Details about the 144,000 Jewish witnesses
- The ministry of the three angels described
- Vision of Jesus about to harvest and judge

Midpoint of the Tribulation

- Two witnesses killed in Jerusalem, then resurrected
- Massive earthquake in Jerusalem will destroy ten percent of the city and kill 7,000 people
- Abomination of desecration, antichrist demands worship
- Jews flee from Jerusalem to Bozra/Petra for protection
- Mark of the beast system enforced
- The three angels announce:
    1. The gospel
    2. Babylon's coming destruction

3. Warning against worshipping the beast, his image, or taking his mark

Seven Last Plagues/Bowl Judgments (Revelation 15–16)

- Another vision of what's taking place in heaven's throne room
- First bowl—festering sores on those with the mark
- Second bowl—seas turn to blood killing all sea life
- Third bowl—all rivers turned to blood
- Fourth bowl—sun scorches people (possibly due to earth's ozone layer and atmosphere breaking down, coronal mass ejections, and/or solar flares)
- Fifth bowl—selective pitch-black darkness over the beast's kingdom
- Sixth bowl—Euphrates River completely dries up, making a passageway for Asian leaders/armies to cross
- Three demonic lying and persuasive spirits influence the leaders of the world to join the antichrist and attack Israel
- Seventh bowl—massive storm and a massive global earthquake, the worst the world has ever seen
- followed by a plague of hail featuring 100-pound hailstones

Babylon Destroyed (Revelation 17–19:10)

- Antichrist's kingdom, capitol, and aspirations collapse
- All that is left for the antichrist is to finish his attempt to destroy Israel and the Jews with the nations of the world that have gathered with him

Jesus Returns (Revelation 19:11-21)

- Jesus breaks through our dimension riding a war horse with the armies of heaven following to defeat the antichrist and judge the nations

- The eight stages of Armageddon (according to Old Testament prophets and Revelation)

    1. Gathering of world armies at Armageddon
    2. Babylon destroyed by God
    3. Jerusalem attacked
    4. Antichrist's armies attack Jewish people hidden in Bozrah
    5. Israel turns to the Lord corporately
    6. Jewish people rescued by Jesus
    7. Antichrist's armies destroyed in Valley of Jehoshaphat
    8. Jesus descends to the Mount of Olives in victory

Millennial Kingdom (Revelation 20)

- Satan thrown into abyss and sealed for 1,000 years
- Jesus establishes the kingdom, ruling from Jerusalem
- Satan released for one last battle
- Satan cast into Lake of Fire forever
- The Great White Throne Judgment (final) of unbelievers occurs

New Heavens/New Earth/Eternal State (Revelation 21–22)

- New heavens and new earth created
- New Jerusalem descends from heaven to the new earth
- Eden is restored and evil is destroyed once and for all

The Threefold Application of the Seven Churches

There is a very interesting aspect of the seven churches that I'd like to point out. In contrast to other letters of the New Testament, which were written by Paul, here we have Jesus himself giving words of encouragement and warning. Also, right at the beginning of chapter 1, we are told specifically that this is a book of prophecy. Prophecy foretells the future.

Many passages of prophetic Scripture have an immediate or literal application, possible secondary applications, and ultimately a broader prophetic fulfillment.

With that in mind, I'd like to highlight some fascinating facts about the churches John addressed in Revelation 2 and 3. Many prophecy experts agree that the seven churches were not only literal churches, but that they also prophetically foreshadow seven distinct church periods—and that they are also part of the prophecy of this book.

Literal Application

The seven churches in Revelation 2–3 were seven literal churches. They were all located in different areas of modern-day Turkey. The warnings and commendations given to these churches were relevant to the people who were part of those churches at that specific time.

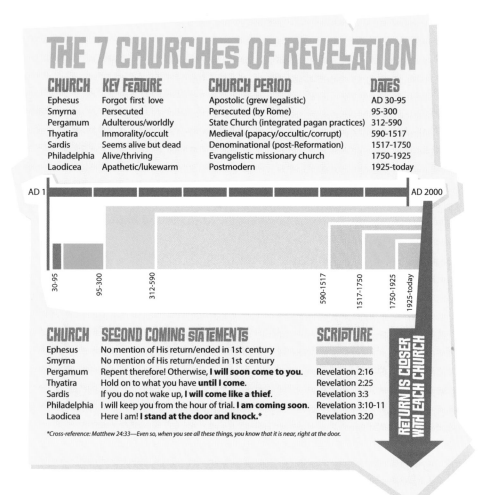

THE 7 CHURCHES OF REVELATION

CHURCH	KEY FEATURE	CHURCH PERIOD	DATES
Ephesus	Forgot first love	Apostolic (grew legalistic)	AD 30-95
Smyrna	Persecuted	Persecuted (by Rome)	95-300
Pergamum	Adulterous/worldly	State Church (integrated pagan practices)	312-590
Thyatira	Immorality/occult	Medieval (papacy/occultic/corrupt)	590-1517
Sardis	Seems alive but dead	Denominational (post-Reformation)	1517-1750
Philadelphia	Alive/thriving	Evangelistic missionary church	1750-1925
Laodicea	Apathetic/lukewarm	Postmodern	1925-today

AD 1   AD 2000

30-95   95-300   312-590   590-1517   1517-1750   1750-1925   1925-today

CHURCH	SECOND COMING STATEMENTS	SCRIPTURE
Ephesus	No mention of His return/ended in 1st century	
Smyrna	No mention of His return/ended in 1st century	
Pergamum	Repent therefore! Otherwise, **I will soon come to you.**	Revelation 2:16
Thyatira	Hold on to what you have **until I come.**	Revelation 2:25
Sardis	If you do not wake up, **I will come like a thief.**	Revelation 3:3
Philadelphia	I will keep you from the hour of trial. **I am coming soon.**	Revelation 3:10-11
Laodicea	Here I am! **I stand at the door and knock.***	Revelation 3:20

*Cross-reference: Matthew 24:33—Even so, when you see all these things, you know that it is near, right at the door.

RETURN IS CLOSER WITH EACH CHURCH

Secondary Application

The warnings and commendations to the seven churches also highlight characteristics that can be found in churches at any given time in history. The principles presented by Jesus can help believers evaluate churches, and even themselves. In this case, Revelation 2–3 can help serve as guardrails and guiding principles to help churches stay the course and remain faithful to the Lord until he comes again.

Prophetic Application

Finally, the seven churches may also represent seven periods of church history between John's time and the beginning of the tribulation. Some early church leaders believed this would be the case, and history has borne it out as we look in the rearview mirror as well as the church in our day. The strengths, weaknesses, cultural conditions, and chronology of the seven literal churches John addressed very closely mirror those of the seven chronological stages of church history from John's time until today.

Keep in mind that you will find all seven types of churches in each of the seven periods, but at the same time, a careful study of church history shows that each period has been dominated by one type of church. These seven periods of church history have occurred in the same order that John addressed the literal churches in Revelation 2–3. Not all prophecy experts agree on the exact dates or descriptions, but there is a broad consensus about the fact seven periods of church history have unfolded through time since Revelation was written.

Symbolism in Revelation

Sometimes we find clear figures of speech in Scripture. It's obvious they should not be interpreted literally. For example, Jesus frequently used hyperbole in his parables as he talked about things like a camel fitting through the eye of a needle or pointing out a speck of dirt in someone else's eye when we have a plank in our own eye.

Other seemingly confusing passages can be better understood simply by studying the broader context. And still other passages can be better understood by looking for earlier uses of the word or symbol. This is known as "interpreting scripture with scripture" and this method helps us understand the symbolism found in many of the prophetic passages of the Bible. Such is the case with the symbolism in Revelation.

All of the symbols in Revelation first appear somewhere else in Scripture, or the meaning of the symbol is given in the immediate context. This is very important. We can look for earlier precedents of a word or symbol and allow them to inform our understanding of symbols found in Revelation. People get into trouble when they bring their own ideas into what the symbols mean. We need to let Scripture, logic, and the Holy Spirit be our guide.

There are seven basic categories of symbols that show up in Revelation: animals, colors, earthly objects, celestial objects, man-made objects, people, and numbers. We read about symbols such as the seven lamp stands, the beast rising out of the sea, a beast with seven heads and ten horns, a woman riding a beast, the seven seals, the seven scrolls, the seven bowls, the four horsemen of the apocalypse, and the lamb seen in heaven's throne room. Those are just a few examples.

As you study Revelation, you can have confidence that the symbols have a specific, discernible meaning. Once a symbol is understood, this clarity brings fresh meaning to the text and practical insight into what will take place during the endtimes.

Time to Dig In

While the book of Revelation is simpler than most people think, it can also keep you busy for a lifetime. My point in this chapter is not that you can grasp everything there is to know about the book of Revelation with an overview like this one. Rather, my goal has been to strip away the stereotypes that make the book *seem* inaccessible and provide a few principles for getting a better understanding of Revelation.

Now, it's up to you to use these newfound principles as study tools to help you dig deeper into Bible prophecy. Remember, this is God's love letter to you, and you'll discover something new each time you read his supernatural words. He wants you to know what is going to take place. He also wants you to know when that time is drawing near.

With that in mind, let's take a closer look at the signs of the end times. In the next seven chapters (a fitting number for a book on Bible prophecy, eh?) we will review seven key categories of signs we can look for to see whether we are nearing the time of our Lord's return. Buckle your seatbelt!

PART 4:

SO WHERE ARE WE NOW?

CHAPTER 13

The Super Sign—Israel

The LORD gave another message to Jeremiah. He said, "Have you noticed what people are saying? 'The LORD chose Judah and Israel and then abandoned them!'" They are sneering and saying that Israel is not worthy to be counted as a nation. But this is what the LORD says: I would no more reject my people than I would change my laws that govern night and day, earth and sky.

JEREMIAH 33:23-25 (NLT)

Before we dive into the main topic of this chapter, I want to make a bold statement and it is this: Jesus expects his followers to know when his return is near. We are told over and over again to watch, to stay alert, and to stay awake.

A few years ago, I began to sense things were acutely shifting toward long-prophesied end-time conditions. The scary global events I referenced in chapter 1 were getting my attention. Yes, evil and conflict have always been a part of this fallen world, but things seemed to be getting worse—globally. Knowing that emotions can send people to wrong conclusions, I decided first to see what the experts were saying. I wanted to get the opinions of theologians whom I considered to be solid, proven, nonsensationalistic, heavily credentialed, and—most importantly—walking closely with the Lord in humility and integrity.

What I found was astounding. Every trusted source I checked implied or boldly proclaimed their conviction—based on Scripture and current events—that we are fast approaching or currently in the season of the Lord's return. Several adamantly believe that we are the generation that will experience the rapture.

I know, I know—people have been saying that for years; or at least since the 1970s when author Hal Lindsey's book, *The Late Great Planet Earth,* burst onto the scene. I get it, and I understand the reservation. My point is, these aren't the opinions of obscure lone-wolf personalities who claimed to have had some special revelation, or some strange esoteric method for setting dates for the end of the world. These were solid, highly respected experts who have been studying Scripture and world events for decades and have a clear sense that the end-time events described in the Bible are likely closer to us than most people think.

BILLY GRAHAM, FAMOUS EVANGELIST, MINISTER, AUTHOR

"What a time to take the news of the day in one hand and the Bible in the other and watch the unfolding of the great drama of the ages come together. This is an exciting and thrilling time to be alive...It is not just Christians that sense something is about to happen. The world knows that things cannot go on as they are. History has reached an impasse. This world is on a collision course. Something is about to give. With increasing frequency, commentators from secular media speak of Armageddon."

(The Reason for My Hope, Billy Graham, Thomas Nelson, 2013, pg. 175)

DR. CHUCK MISSLER, AUTHOR, SPEAKER, FOUNDER OF KOINONIA INSTITUTE

"It appears that we are presently being plunged into a period of time that the Bible says more about than any other period of history—including the events of the New Testament."

(Prophecy 20/20, Dr. Chuck Missler, Thomas Nelson, Inc., 2006, pg. 2)

DWIGHT PENTECOST, THEOLOGIAN, PROFESSOR AT DALLAS THEOLOGICAL SEMINARY (DIED IN 2014)

"Will you imagine please, a platform that is shut off by a curtain that's drawn? There's a lot of activity going on behind that drawn curtain. If there's a little crack between the bottom of the curtain and the floor, you can see feet rushing around, you can hear furniture being moved, you can hear things going on. You can't see, but you know that the stage manager is in control and is directing to make sure that every person and every prop essential to that drama is in place. I think that's the day in which we're living."

(The Road to Armageddon, Charles R. Swindoll, John F. Walvoord, J. Dwight Pentecost, Thomas Nelson, 1999, pg. 100)

DR. TIM LAHAYE, PASTOR, SPEAKER, AUTHOR
(Best known for the Left Behind series, died 2016)

"We have more reason than any generation before us to believe He will come in our generation."

(Are We Living in the End Times? by Tim LaHaye and Jerry B. Jenkins, Tyndale House, 1999, pg. 6)

THOMAS ICE, EXECUTIVE DIRECTOR OF THE PRE-TRIB RESEARCH CENTER
(on the campus of Liberty University in Lynchburg, VA)

"We believe that God is now setting the stage for the next era of history, which is known as the Tribulation. There are signs around us that give evidence of this."

(Charting the End Times, Tim LaHaye and Thomas Ice, Harvest House Publishers, 2001, pg. 118)

RON RHODES, AUTHOR, SPEAKER

"Do I believe we are living in the season of the Lord's return, and if so, why? Yes. I say this because of what I call the 'convergence factor.' Not only has Israel come together as a nation again, as prophesied (Ezekiel 26–27), but a number of ancient prophecies of the end times seem to be converging in our day."

(Living on Borrowed Time, Dr. David Reagan with Ron Rhodes, Lamb & Lion Ministries, 2013, pg. 76)

If you'll recall from chapter 1, we saw how Jesus chastised the religious leaders and the crowds of people for not being able to discern the signs of their day (Matthew 16:3; Luke 12:56), and how Hebrews 10:25 explicitly tells us we can "see the day approaching." Then in chapter 11, we looked at Jesus's second-longest recorded teaching, which was prompted by his disciples' questions about the signs that would signal the end of the age.

But Won't Jesus Come Like a Thief?

Even statements like "No man knows the day or the hour" and "The day of the Lord will come like a thief in the night," though they remind us we shouldn't attempt to set dates, weren't given to discourage us from watching for the general signs of Christ's eventual return. The opposite is actually true. When viewed in context, those two passages call us to "keep watch" and "be awake." Let's look at them more carefully:

> *About that day or hour no one knows, not even the angels in heaven, nor the Son, but only the Father.* As it was in the days of Noah, so it will be at the coming of the Son of Man. For in the days before the flood, people were eating and drinking, marrying and giving in marriage, up to the day Noah entered the ark; and they knew nothing about what would happen until the flood came and took them all away. That is how it will be at the coming of the Son of Man. Two men will be in the field; one will be taken and the other left. Two women will be grinding with a hand mill; one will be taken and the other left. *Therefore keep watch, because you do not know on what day your Lord will come* (Matthew 24:36-42, emphasis mine).

> Now, brothers and sisters, *about times and dates we do not need to write to you,* for you know very well that *the day of the Lord will come like a thief in the night.* While people are saying, "Peace and safety," destruction will come on them suddenly, as labor pains on a pregnant woman, and they will not escape. *But you, brothers and sisters, are not in darkness so that this day should surprise you like a thief.* You are all children of the light and children of the day. We do not belong to the night or to the darkness. So then, let us not be like others, who are asleep, but let us be awake and sober (1 Thessalonians 5:1-6, emphasis mine).

Read carefully, these two passages demonstrate that the unbelieving world, those still caught in darkness, will definitely be caught off guard. But those of us who are "children of the light" will absolutely *not* be caught off guard. We are told to watch. Watch for what? The signs of his coming. We are told that "this day" (the day of the Lord, or the tribulation period) will *not* surprise us like a thief in the night.

The Matthew 24 passage also says the period leading up to the rapture will be like the days of Noah. Noah knew when his massive boat project was almost completed. He knew the time was near. He watched the evil grow all around him. He didn't know the day or hour, but he knew the season and saw the stage fully set. Prior to the rapture, conditions will be similar. Most of the world will be caught completely by surprise even though they have heard the warnings. Today, scoffers think we are crazy. To the people of Noah's day, Noah's boat project seemed insane—until the flood came.

It's also interesting to note that the phrases "like a thief in the night" and "no man knows the day or the hour" are ancient Jewish idioms. The Israelite priests were instructed in Leviticus 6:8-13 to wear linen clothing and keep the altar fires burning all night. The high priest (a figure or type of Christ) would check on the priests to see if they fell asleep while on watch. If so, he would set their extremely flammable linen clothes on fire and they would leave naked and ashamed.

> Revelation 16:15—Look, I come like a thief! Blessed is the one who stays awake and remains clothed, so as not to go naked and be shamefully exposed.

The phrase "no man knows the day or the hour" is an idiom related to the Feast of Trumpets. It was the only one of the seven Jewish feasts that began on a new moon. Because this feast begins on a new moon, "no man knows the day or the hour" of its exact beginning. This idiom, specific to the Feast of Trumpets, shows up in language concerning the rapture (Matthew 24:36; Mark 13:32). In order for this feast to begin, two witnesses—two priests given this duty—had to agree that they saw only a small sliver of the moon. If the night sky was covered with clouds, they would have to wait until the sky cleared, or wait until the next evening. Once both witnesses confirmed the new moon, a shofar was sounded to officially begin the Feast of Trumpets. Then signal fires were lit on high mountains and word spread to the whole Jewish community that the feast had officially begun. When it came to starting the Feast of Trumpets, then, it was true that no man knew the day or the hour ahead of time. But that does not mean we can't know the general season.

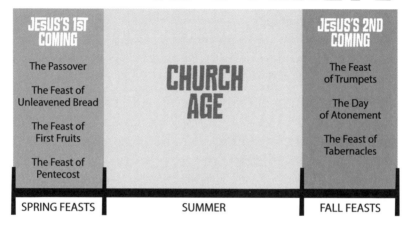

THE LORD'S FEASTS

JESUS'S 1ST COMING	CHURCH AGE	JESUS'S 2ND COMING
The Passover		The Feast of Trumpets
The Feast of Unleavened Bread		The Day of Atonement
The Feast of First Fruits		The Feast of Tabernacles
The Feast of Pentecost		
SPRING FEASTS	SUMMER	FALL FEASTS

I say all of that to lay some firm groundwork before we look at specific end-time signs. I want you to feel secure knowing that the endeavor to understand end-time signs is a legitimate area of Bible study, and that it is more relevant today than at any other time in history. It should by no means be the only thing we study, and we must stick to Scripture as our sole source of authority. That said, let's look at the first key sign to consider.

Why Israel Is the Super Sign

Many prophecy experts call Israel "the super sign." They refer to it this way for two key reasons. First, all the other end-time signs hinge on this one sign. No other sign of the end could occur until Israel became a nation again. Second, experts call Israel the super sign because of the sheer magnitude of this sign coming to pass. It is statistically impossible to predict this sign with all of its details and necessary preconditions, and have it fulfilled as it has been in our modern era.

No other ancient people group in the history of the world has been spread all over the world, kicked out of nation after nation, yet maintained their national identity, customs, and ancient language. Just as impressive is the fact that after 1,878 years, the Jewish people have returned to their homeland in large numbers and have become one of the world's strongest and wealthiest nations.

JEWISH DIASPORA (ISRAEL'S DISPERSION)

1878 YEARS (AD 70-1948)

240+ YEARS
AGE OF AMERICA

These details (and many others) were all predicted in Scripture thousands of years ago. Consider Jeremiah 16:14-15, which was written 2,600 years ago:

> "However, the days are coming," declares the LORD, "when it will no longer be said, 'As surely as the LORD lives, who brought the Israelites up out of Egypt,' but it will be said, 'As surely as the LORD lives, *who brought the Israelites up* out of the land of the north and *out of all the countries* where he had banished them.' For *I will restore them to the land I gave their ancestors*" (emphasis mine).

Did you catch that? That Israel became a nation again was a greater miracle than Moses parting the Red Sea. Let that sink in a moment and think about the billions of details that had to occur between AD 70, when the Romans destroyed Jerusalem, and 1948, when Israel became a nation again. This one single sign should absolutely floor us when we think about it.

QUICK FACT: DID YOU KNOW...
... that every one of the Old Testament prophets except Jonah predicted the rebirth of the nation of Israel?

A study of the people of Israel will show that prophecy has been fulfilled in many ways. This also explains why Satan has used evil rulers in every age to mistreat and attempt to eliminate the Jews altogether. From Pharaoh to Mordecai to Hitler to today's terrorists and radical Islamic states, there has been a millennia-long attempt to destroy the Jewish race. Initially, I was going to include a list of periods of Jewish persecution through the ages, but found it would triple the length of this chapter. No people group has been persecuted like the Jewish people.

Why? Because the Scriptures and the Messiah came from her, and because end-times prophecy requires a return of the Jews to their land, then to their Messiah, just in time for the millennial kingdom! God said Israel is the "apple of his eye" (Zechariah 2:8). The worst way to hurt someone is to hurt their kids. Satan still thinks he can win if he destroys the most essential element to end-times prophecy—the Jewish people.

Prophecy's Timepiece

Since the fulfillment of all end-time prophecies hinge on the nation of Israel being in existence, the reborn nation is referred to by many prophecy teach-

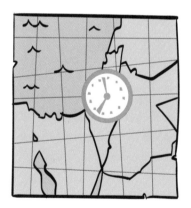

ers as end-time prophecy's timepiece. It has even been stated that Israel is the clock, Jerusalem is the hour hand, and the Temple Mount in Old Jerusalem is the second hand. Bestselling author and prophecy teacher Joel Rosenberg calls the Temple Mount the "epicenter" (also the name of one of his award-winning books) of Bible prophecy.

Israel's rebirth is the main aspect of this super sign, but there are many other end-time signs associated with it. Several prophecies regarding events leading up to, and after, her rebirth in our modern era (beginning in the late 1800s) were predicted in Scripture.

The Backdrop

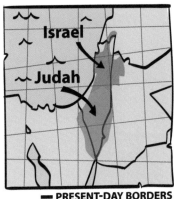

— PRESENT-DAY BORDERS

In the Old Testament, God warned Israel of judgment if the people continued to stray from him. Because they continued to rebel, God poured out his judgment. First, in 772 BC, the northern kingdom of Israel was taken captive by Assyria. Then, in 586 BC, the southern kingdom of Judah was taken into captivity by the Babylonians. God sent multiple prophets to each nation prior to their judgment, calling them to turn back to the Lord, but they refused.

After 70 years of captivity, God allowed his people to return to their homeland (the first time). As time went on, they drifted from the Lord again and most rejected Christ at his first coming. God then allowed the Romans to destroy Jerusalem in AD 70, and the Jewish people were scattered all over the world—initially in nearby regions, then as the centuries ticked by, globally. They were rejected and persecuted at various times and in various ways in the nations they attempted to settle in. This was the second, and much more severe, dispersion.

With that backdrop in mind, consider these prophecies from more than 2,600 years ago:

> Deuteronomy 28:64—"The LORD will scatter you among all peoples, from one end of the earth to the other."

> Ezekiel 37:21-22—"This is what the Sovereign LORD says: I will take the Israelites out of the nations where they have gone. I will gather them from all around and bring them back into their own land. I will make them *one nation* in the land, on the mountains of Israel" (emphasis mine).

> Isaiah 11:11—"In that day the Lord will reach out his hand a *second time* to bring back the remnant of his people" (emphasis mine).

The Winds of Prophecy Begin to Blow

THEODOR HERZL
1860–1904

In the late 1800s, Theodor Herzl, the father of the Zionist movement (1860–1904), began to call for a Jewish state and began challenging his fellow Jews to return to their homeland. At the 1897 Zionist Conference in Basel, Switzerland, he stated that he believed the Jewish state would come into existence within 50 years.

The Ottoman Turks, who controlled Israel's ancient homeland at the beginning of the twentieth century, picked the wrong side in World War I. When they lost, the French and British governments divided up the land of the former Ottoman Empire. The British government was given oversight of Palestine. As a result, on November 2, 1917, the Balfour Declaration, a public statement by the British government, announced support for the establishment of a national home for the Jewish people in Palestine. Jews and Christians who held to a literal interpretation of Scripture saw this as the first real sign of Israel's reestablishment, and along with it, the first sign that the world was entering the end times.

Thirty years later, after the Holocaust during World War II, the world softened a bit toward the suffering Jewish people, and on November 29, 1947, the United Nations voted to create a state for them. Then on May 14, 1948, the modern-day nation of Israel was officially born. Having barely survived the Holocaust and having experienced persecution everywhere they went, the Jewish people declared themselves a nation in a single day.

> Isaiah 66:7-8—Before she goes into labor, she gives birth; before the pains come upon her, she delivers a son. Who has ever heard of such things? Who has ever seen things like this? Can a country be born in a day or a nation be brought forth in a moment?

The United States of America officially recognized Israel's sovereignty that same day. The following day, Great Britain relinquished its official oversight of

Palestine, and immediately, Israel—surrounded by enemies on all sides—was attacked by Egypt, Iraq, Transjordan, Syria, Lebanon, Saudi Arabia, and Yemen.

Since then, Israel has faced no less than 11 wars or major conflicts—in every case, the recipient of attacks from her neighbors. And after every one of those attacks, she has grown militarily stronger.

The Six-Day War of 1967 was nothing short of a miracle. In her 1948 war for independence, Israel held her enemies at bay for two months and survived. In 1967, she defeated enemies on all sides in a mere six days. Like David and Goliath, Israel—a tiny country the size of New Jersey— beat a group of much larger foes attacking from the north and the south. It is clear that God's hand was protecting her. And during the Six-Day War, Israel gained more land, including Jerusalem and the Temple Mount.

Zechariah 12:6—On that day I will make the clans of Judah like a firepot in a woodpile, like a flaming torch among sheaves. They will consume all the surrounding peoples right and left, but Jerusalem will remain intact in her place.

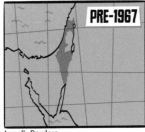  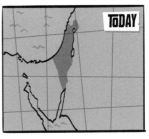

Israel's Borders

In 1900, there were approximately 40,000 Jewish people in the land. After World War II, there were around 600,000. Today there are more Jewish people living in Israel than the six million who were lost in the Holocaust. No other ancient people group from the days of the Old Testament has known a similar dispersion and rebirth.

The God of History and Time

Israel is seen as the super sign because all end-time signs and conditions require Israel to first be reestablished as a nation. The fulfillment of this single all-important sign is key to the eventual fulfillment of every other end-time sign. There are scores of other related signs that could not occur until after Israel was reborn. The odds of this monumental fulfillment occurring by sheer chance is impossible. This serves as an incredible confirmation that the God of the Bible is wholly sovereign over history and time.

CHAPTER 14

The Geopolitical Signs

There will be signs in the sun, in the moon, and in the stars; and on earth distress of nations, with perplexity.

LUKE 21:25 (NKJV)

During the 2003 invasion of Iraq, when US troops took the city of Baghdad, I remember watching a somewhat comical news briefing given by Iraq's information minister. Behind him, smoke was rising from the city. In other footage, US tanks and armored personnel carriers were rolling into central Baghdad, and a large statue of Saddam Hussein was being torn down. Even so, the reality-defying information minister stood in front of news cameras and declared that American infidels had not established any presence at all in the city of Baghdad. His denial reminds me of the attitude that many people in our day have toward the chaos taking place all around us.

Frightening events are the result of living in a fallen world, but so many developments have taken place in recent years that we can no longer ignore them or chalk them up to cyclical instability.

So what can we learn from Bible prophecy about the geopolitical landscape of our day? Can we shake off our reality-distortion glasses and look at the ominous conditions of our day through the lens of Scripture? Are these geopolitical conditions signs that we are nearing the end of the age?

The Picture on the Box

The primary key to successfully assembling a puzzle is the all-important picture on the top of the box. Without it, there is no way to make sense of a chaotic pile of puzzle pieces. Fortunately for us, the Bible provides a clear picture. Here's a prophetic snapshot of what the last-days geopolitical puzzle should look like.

Mideast Meltdown

During the tribulation, there will be a series of horrific wars that will escalate and eventually culminate in what is commonly known as the Battle of Armageddon. Scripture also tells us about two other wars that will occur before (or very early in) the tribulation period.

The Bible indicates that Israel will first be attacked by her immediate border neighbors (Psalm 83), then later by an outer ring of nations that do not share a border with Israel. This second attack will be led by a Russian-Arab alliance (Ezekiel 38–39). For these reasons, we should expect to see increasing instability in the Mideast, beginning with Israel's rebirth as a nation, then leading up to (and all the way through) the tribulation period.

Psalm 83 War

> Psalm 83:3-5—With cunning they conspire against your people; they plot against those you cherish. "Come," they say, "let us destroy them as a nation, so that Israel's name is remembered no more." With one mind they plot together; they form an alliance against you.

If you'll recall from the previous chapter, as soon as Israel was declared a nation in 1948, she was attacked by her Arab neighbors. In the years that followed, there were several additional major conflicts with the surrounding Arab countries. During these conflicts—most notably the Six-Day War of 1967—Israel was attacked by the nations listed in Psalm 83 for the reasons stated in that passage. Israel's enemies were also soundly defeated and humiliated, just as described in Psalm 83.

"The armies of Egypt, Jordan, Syria and Lebanon are poised on the borders of Israel...to face the challenge, while standing behind us are the armies of Iraq, Algeria, Kuwait, Sudan and the whole Arab nation...We have reached the stage of serious action and not of more declarations."

—PRESIDENT GAMAL ABDEL NASSER OF EGYPT, MAY 30, 1967

"The existence of Israel is an error which must be rectified. This is our opportunity to wipe out the ignominy which has been with us since 1948. Our goal is clear — to wipe Israel off the map."

—PRESIDENT AREF OF IRAQ, MAY 31, 1967

When you look at the list of nations listed in Psalm 83, they mirror the modern-day countries that have already attacked Israel.

It's important to note here that not all prophecy experts agree on the interpretation of Psalm 83. Some believe the events described there have yet to occur, while others suggest it is merely a song of prayer. Still others believe the happenings in Psalm 83 are part of the Ezekiel 38 war (described below), or that they are part of the Armageddon campaign, which will take place at the end of the tribulation. It is my conviction that the Psalm 83 war has already been fulfilled, particularly in the 1967 Six-Day War, though I'm not dogmatic about it.

PSALM 83 NATIONS

AND THEIR MODERN-DAY EQUIVALENTS

ANCIENT NAME	MODERN NAME
ISHMAELITES	EGYPT
HAGARENES	EGYPT
ASSUR	IRAQ and SYRIA
EDOM	JORDAN
MOAB	JORDAN
AMMON	JORDAN
AMALEK	JORDAN
LOT	JORDAN
GEBAL	LEBANON
TYRE	LEBANON
PHILISTINES	PLO
TYRE	PLO

As I mentioned, Psalm 83 describes the same countries, intentions, and outcome as the Six-Day War. I also don't think it was a coincidence that Israel fought for six days (against insurmountable odds, like the matchup between David and Goliath) and rested on the seventh. This seems to have the hallmarks of God's activity, mirroring the pattern whereby he created the world in six days and rested on the seventh. In any case, the stage is now set for the next major war against Israel—the Ezekiel 38 war.

Ezekiel 38 War

This future war is also known as the war of Gog and Magog. The verses below describe a leader called Gog (a title, or more likely, the evil spirit who influences the leader) who comes from the land of Magog. Magog was a grandson of Noah (Genesis 10:2), and his descendants migrated north of the Black Sea in what is modern-day Russia. There are some prophecy teachers who believe the antichrist is going to be a Muslim, and they have proposed that Magog is modern-day Turkey. But I believe the traditional view of Russia as Magog makes more sense and is the correct view. In either case, we see the stage being set in our day unlike at any other time.

> Ezekiel 38:1-4—"The word of the LORD came to me: 'Son of man, set your face against Gog, of the land of Magog, the chief prince of Meshek and Tubal; prophesy against him and say: "This is what the Sovereign Lord says: I am against you, Gog, chief prince of *Meshek* and *Tubal.* I will *turn you around*, put *hooks in your jaws* and bring

you out with your whole army"""" (emphasis mine; many prophecy experts believe these are the modern-day Russian cities of Moscow and Tobolsk).

Ezekiel 38:8-9—"After many days you will be visited. In the *latter years* you will come into the *land of those brought back from the sword and gathered from many people* on the mountains of *Israel, which had long been desolate*; they were *brought out of the nations*, and now *all of them dwell safely*. You will ascend, coming like a storm, covering the land like a cloud, you and all your troops and *many peoples with you*" (NKJV, emphasis mine).

Ezekiel 39:2—"I will turn you around and drag you along. I will bring you from *the far north* and send you *against the mountains of Israel*" (emphasis mine).

For the first time since her rebirth (after the land was desolate for 1,800 years and the Jewish people were almost destroyed during World War II), Israel is enjoying a state of peace with her sovereign neighbors. Israel currently has peace treaties with Jordan and Egypt, and has—for the first time in history, at the time of this writing—begun building a regional partnership with Saudi Arabia.

Because Iran is predominantly Shia and is developing nuclear capabilities, Sunni nations such as Saudi Arabia are—surprisingly—turning to Israel to help build an alliance against the threat posed by Iran. Also, two of Israel's traditional enemies—Iraq and Syria—are no longer in a position to threaten her after years of war, civil war, and the instability caused by the Arab Spring uprisings and ISIS.

QUICK FACT: DID YOU KNOW...

since the death of Muhammad in the seventh century, Sunni and Shia Muslims have fought with each other over who should have succeeded him? The Sunnis believe it should be his father-in-law. The Shia believe it should have been his cousin/son-in-law.

Iran funds proxy terrorist organizations like Hamas and Hezbollah, which have harassed Israel from the Gaza region and the neighboring nation of Lebanon.

But in terms of sovereign bordering nations, Israel exists more securely than at any time since her rebirth. She also has the strongest intelligence capabilities and the strongest military in the region.

But the ominous elements for this distinct end-time war have been maneuvering into position since the beginning of the Syrian civil war. In recent years, prophecy students have watched the 2,600-year-old prophesied "Gog and Magog" alliance take shape. On November 1, 2015, Iran's ambassador to Russia stated that a new chapter in relations between Iran and Russia had begun. This included a bilateral trade agreement between the two former enemies as well as military cooperation in Syria, and Russian support of Iran's nuclear aspirations.

At the time of writing this chapter, ISIS is all but defeated and the Syrian civil war is simmering down, and Russia and Iran have long-term military bases set up in Syria—making public their plans for a permanent presence there. Making matters even more interesting, Russia has taken the lead on "patrolling" the southern portion of Syria—just north of Israel's border, and Iran has declared it wants to establish a direct route from Iran all the way to Israel. Russia and Iran have also strengthened their partnership with Turkey, which until recently was a Western-friendly nation with strong ties to the European Union.

Now Turkey, with its growing authoritarianism under President Recep Tayyip Erdogan, has shifted dramatically. Turkey has grown increasingly anti-Western and anti-Jewish just at the time when all three former-rival countries (Russia, Iran, Turkey) have been drawn into the power vacuum to cement their footprint in Syria in the aftermath of the Syrian civil war. In November 2017, Russian leader Vladimir Putin hosted a summit with his Turkish and Iranian counterparts to plan their future role in the Mideast, and specifically in Syria.

EZEKIEL 38 NATIONS
AND THEIR MODERN-DAY EQUIVALENTS

ANCIENT NAME	MODERN NAME
MAGOG	RUSSIA, CENTRAL ASIA
ROSH	RUSSIA
MESHECH	RUSSIA
TUBAL	RUSSIA OR TURKEY
PERSIA	IRAN
CUSH	ETHIOPIA, SUDAN
LUD	LIBYA, ALGERIA
GOMER	TURKEY
TOGARMAH	TURKEY, CENTRAL ASIA

These countries have formed an unprecedented alliance with other Arab/Muslim countries (all of which hate Israel) that exactly match the confederation that is predicted to attack Israel in the "latter years."

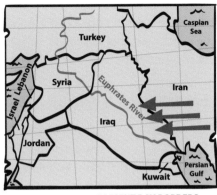

PRESENT-DAY BORDERS

A European Union

In chapter 10 of this book, we learned about Nebuchadnezzar's vision of the statue as chronicled for us in Daniel 2. Let's go back to Daniel 2 and take a closer look at something rather curious. After four sequential world empires, with each empire taking over the previous empire's land and resources, the pattern changes. Notice the details in the verses below.

> Daniel 2:40-45—"Finally, there will be a fourth kingdom, strong as iron—for iron breaks and smashes everything—and as iron breaks things to pieces, so it will crush and break all the others. Just as you saw that the feet and toes were partly of baked clay and partly of iron, *so this will be a divided kingdom; yet it will have some of the strength of iron in it*, even as you saw iron mixed with clay. As the toes were partly iron and partly clay, so *this kingdom will be partly strong and partly brittle*. And just as you saw the iron mixed with baked clay, *so the people will be a mixture and will not remain united*, any more than iron mixes with clay" (emphasis mine).

Instability

After the fourth kingdom, the pattern whereby a new empire conquered a previous one stops. At this point, we find that the legs of the statue break apart into a mixture of strong iron and weak clay in the feet and down to the toes. In other words, the empire will break into a weak union of smaller nation-states, and this weak coalition will continue into the tribulation, when ten elite rulers take over the leadership of the empire or possibly the entire world.

The European Union fits the biblical model well for several reasons. For example, Greece and Italy are deep in debt and are draining the wealth of nations such as Germany. The sudden influx of millions of Syrian refugees, many of whom will not assimilate into European culture because of their Muslim background, has further weakened the European Union. These and many other factors are bringing greater instability to the union.

A Growing Push Toward Globalism

Behind the scenes of the economic and geopolitical instability is a growing philosophical and political push toward a one-world government, currency, and religion. I'll cover the first two here, and the third in chapter 16.

Global Government

Beginning with the League of Nations after World War I, there has been a steady stream of influential diplomatic and political organizations pushing for the establishment of a worldwide government body. These organizations include the Council on Foreign Relations, the United Nations, The Club of Rome, the G8, the Bilderberg Group, as well as several well-documented secret societies consisting of various current and previous world leaders, business leaders, scientists, and economists from around the world.

At first that sounds like the plot for a conspiracy-theory Hollywood blockbuster, but if you do a little research, you'll find that it's true. Influential leaders from varying political persuasions—such as George Soros and Henry Kissinger—openly talk about and push for globalism and a new world order.

CLUB OF ROME'S 10 REGIONS

These organizations and influencers have all advocated various initiatives to form a world government, and they have committed billions of dollars toward making those initiatives reality. For example, The Club of Rome has laid out plans showing the world divided into ten regions, with a "head" appointed over each region—exactly what we see described in Revelation chapter 13 and other passages of Scripture.

In 2015, a document known as *The 2030 Agenda for Sustainable Development* was officially adopted by member states of the United Nations. That title makes it sound like a project involving the care and growth of humanity, but this agenda, in fact, is one of the boldest subversive attempts ever made toward setting up a one-world governing authority.

Those who created this agenda have the goal of transforming the world by the year 2030. The language used in the actual document is that it is a "new universal agenda for humanity." Environment, economics, agriculture, gender equality, and several other areas of human life are addressed. Just about every nation in the UN (including the US under former president Obama) has signed onto this agenda.

Ultimately, it is a template for global governance. Here is a description taken directly from the UN's website: "The new agenda seeks to *leave no one behind* and aspires to *transform the world* in which we live. The 2030 Agenda forms the *new global development framework* anchored around *17 Sustainable Development Goals* (SDGs) with a total of 169 targets covering *economic, social development, and environmental protection*" (emphasis mine).

There's no doubt that the UN's push for some type of one-world governing body intersects with what Bible prophecy says will take place in the future. Neither the UN nor the EU are founded on eternal biblical principles. Both are based on humanism and naturalism—apart from any consideration of a creator, a Savior, or a final judge.

A One-World Currency

Revelation 13:16-17 gives us a glimpse of what is to come with regard to economic transactions: "[The antichrist] also forced everyone, small and great, rich and poor, free and slave, to receive a mark on his right hand or on his forehead, *so that no one could buy or sell unless he had the mark*, which is the name of the beast or the number of his name" (emphasis mine).

In chapter 18 we'll talk about the technology needed for a one-world currency, but relevant to this chapter is the fact that we are already seeing a growing push for a one-world currency and a cashless system. In order for the mark technology described in Revelation 13:16-17 to be possible, the groundwork for this system will have had to be laid prior to the tribulation period.

The Great Recession of 2008 demonstrated just how interconnected world economies are today. Most financial transactions are cashless. Completely digital cryptocurrencies—such as bitcoin—are proliferating and causing governments to begin looking at ways to bring cryptocurrencies under the control of the global financial system. It's really only a matter of time before we have a one-world currency.

The Rise of the Kings of the East

Another significant prophetic development over the last century has been the rise of the Asian nations. Until recent history, the nations that lie east of the Euphrates River have had little impact on global politics, economic conditions, or military considerations.

Today, China has the world's third-largest economy, which trails the United States and the European Union. China also has almost 1.4 billion citizens, and 3.7 million military personnel. North Korea is an emerging nuclear power with a madman in charge. India and Pakistan both have nuclear weapons, and India has a population of 1.3 billion people with a military of almost 2.6 million personnel.

Daniel 11 and Revelation 9 and 16 inform us that during the tribulation period, rulers and armies from Asia will be major end-time players. In the span of world history, this is a very recent development.

An Omen of Things to Come

These are a few of the current geopolitical conditions of our day. There are many more I had to leave out because there is not enough space to cover them all. But what I've cited above should provide a good snapshot of the end-time picture on top of the puzzle box.

The geopolitical stage-setting we are witnessing today is unprecedented and clearly prophesied in Scripture. Life in our era is busy, and we each have hundreds of things that distract us and give us tunnel vision. However, when we take the time to view the news headlines of the world in light of specific prophecies foretold in Scripture, we can see that changes are taking place that are clearly setting the stage for key end-time events.

I don't see any way that current world conditions could possibly deescalate. In other words, the stage will not be unset. The developments taking place now may speed up or slow down, but at some point, the prophecies regarding the end times will come to pass—and we are watching the stage being set right now.

CHAPTER 15

The Signs of Nature

Nation will rise against nation, and kingdom against kingdom. There will be famines and earthquakes in various places. All these are the beginning of birth pains.

MATTHEW 24:7-8

My wife and I have three children, and though I don't know what it's like personally to go through labor pains, I've witnessed them firsthand. Contractions start out small with long gaps between them. As labor progresses, the contractions increase in duration, intensity, and frequency until finally, the baby is born.

For obvious reasons, my wife and I were rookies when our first child was born. We went to Lamaze classes to learn what to expect, but there's no substitute for actual experience. When our inevitable delivery room visit arrived, I found one of the labor assessment techniques particularly interesting.

So that the doctor could accurately track my wife's labor, sensors were placed on her abdomen. These recorded the frequency and intensity of her contractions. With my artistic bent, I've always found that visual representations of data make more sense to me than a bunch of numbers. Thus I found it interesting that we could watch my wife's contractions on a small screen and a continuous printout.

With our first child, my wife was in labor all through the night. Periodically the doctor would come into the room and examine the printout to make sure the contractions were increasing. He could look back in time, so to speak, to see how labor had progressed.

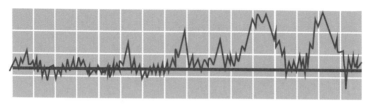

In chapter 11 we took a detailed look at the Olivet Discourse. In that key end-time teaching, Jesus talked about an upheaval of nature (along with other signs) that would increase in frequency and intensity—like birth pains—as his return drew near. We learned that the first major sign signaling history's entrance into the end-time season was a world war.

Jesus said this would be followed by famine, earthquakes, and pestilence. Other clues in the text of the Olivet Discourse let us know that these would occur along with Israel becoming a nation once again.

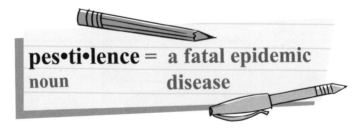

pes•ti•lence = a fatal epidemic
noun   disease

In times past God has used storms, eclipses, earthquakes, stars, drought, locusts, and many other elements of nature to communicate. With the convulsions of nature leading up to the tribulation period, God is again using the signs of nature to inform us that this era is drawing to a close. Eventually, the baby must be born.

Using real data on earthquakes, volcano eruptions, extreme weather events, famine, and disease, we can demonstrate these major signs are shouting like a megaphone as to the nearness of the Lord's return. Just as my wife's contraction printout displayed evidence that her labor was progressing, as we draw closer to the last days, we should expect to see an increase in the severity of natural disasters.

Apart from God, the world's reaction is to freak out and look for man-centered solutions. You can attach various names to these birth pains, such as global warming, or climate change, but nothing will stop the birth pains. There's no such thing as being a little bit pregnant. Ready or not, the baby—at some point—will be born. As we view the conditions of our day, it's clear that the contractions of nature have already begun.

> Isaiah 66:9—"Do I bring to the moment of birth and not give delivery?" says the Lord. "Do I close up the womb when I bring to delivery?" says your God.

The Natural Signs
Earthquakes and Volcanos

Haiti. Japan. Indonesia. Chile. Pakistan. These are some of the places that have experienced major earthquakes in recent memory—earthquakes that caught the world's attention due to their destructive power, resultant tsunamis, and staggering loss of life.

QUICK FACT: DID YOU KNOW...

that the 2004 Indian Ocean 9.3 earthquake and tsunami killed 230,000-280,000 people in 14 countries and caused 100-foot-high waves? It is the third-largest quake ever recorded, and had the longest duration ever recorded (8.3-10 minutes).

As I mentioned in a previous chapter, prophecy expert Tim LaHaye pointed out in his book *Are We Living in the End Times?* that the number of earthquakes worldwide has risen so dramatically that in 2009 the USGS National Earthquake Information Center stopped keeping track of quakes that were smaller than 4.5 in magnitude unless damage or loss of life demanded it.

The most recent official USGS worldwide earthquake chart I could find on the Internet was from 2008. It originated from https://earthquake.usgs.gov/regional/world/historical.php (no longer available). The chart, which I have re-created below, shows clear contraction-like patterns from 1900 to around 1999, followed by a sudden unprecedented exponential curve from 2000–2008. This trend has continued since. I found several articles from 2012 forward which demonstrated that earthquakes have continued to increase in frequency at an extremely fast rate.

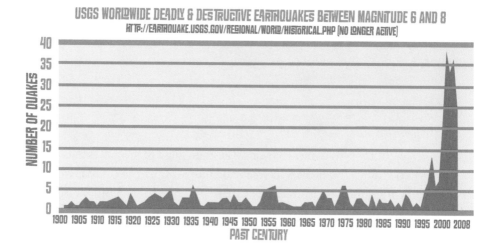

In 2017, a new term made its way into our common vernacular—*earthquake swarms*. At Yellowstone National Park between June 12 and August 2, there were 1,562 earthquakes, with more than 400 of them occurring in the span of a single week.

In Oklahoma, earthquakes have increased exponentially since 2010. Do a quick Internet search for "Oklahoma earthquake chart," and you will find dozens of charts from the USGS, the Oklahoma Geological Survey, and other official sources showing a very similar exponential curve as seen in the chart above.

In 2017, a great film called *The Coming Convergence* was produced by Ingenuity Films. In it, the producers show a global earthquake chart using USGS data of all known earthquakes of the last 100 years that were more than 6.3 on the Richter scale. The producers used only data from quakes registering 6.3 or higher, because that was the lowest level that seismic sensors 100 years ago could pick up from anywhere on the globe. The producers wanted to make sure the data used was 100 percent accurate and that they were comparing apples with apples.

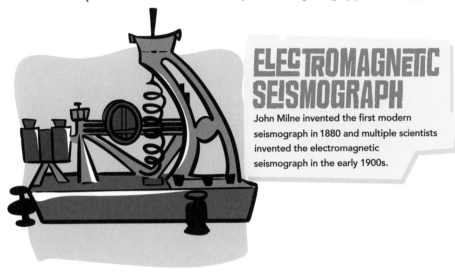

ELECTROMAGNETIC SEISMOGRAPH

John Milne invented the first modern seismograph in 1880 and multiple scientists invented the electromagnetic seismograph in the early 1900s.

The results revealed an unmistakable pattern of birth pains increasing with frequency and intensity as the years progressed. The early 1900s show quakes in the low 6.0-magnitude range. By the mid-1920s, they broke the 8.0 plane. By the late 1940s—over 9.0. By the late 1970s, every year from then until now has stayed above 8.0 with roughly half going over 9.0, and a few times edging close to 10.0 on the Richter scale.

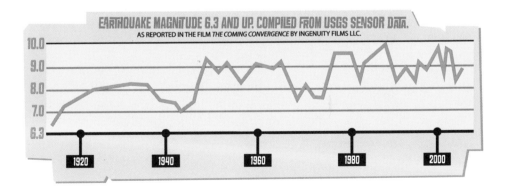

EARTHQUAKE MAGNITUDE 6.3 AND UP. COMPILED FROM USGS SENSOR DATA.
AS REPORTED IN THE FILM *THE COMING CONVERGENCE* BY INGENUITY FILMS LLC.

Another important fact that makes the data in the preceding chart even more compelling is that the power difference between magnitudes is much greater than the chart suggests. Magnitude measures waves on a seismogram, not the actual amount of energy of earthquakes. In terms of energy, one full number difference in magnitude is actually *hundreds* of times stronger and more destructive in terms of actual energy released by an earthquake.

QUICK FACT: DID YOU KNOW...

that a magnitude 8.7 earthquake is 23,000 times stronger than a 5.8 earthquake? It would take 23,000 quakes of a 5.8 magnitude to equal the energy released by one 8.7 quake!

(Source: USGS, https://earthquake.usgs.gov/learn/topics/how_much_bigger.php)

The number and intensity of active volcanos worldwide has followed a similar pattern as earthquakes. No surprise there, because the two are related, but this further demonstrates the accuracy and trustworthiness of the earthquake data. Long-dormant volcanoes are waking up, and we've added yet another geophysical term to our everyday language—the *supervolcano*.

The aforementioned Yellowstone activity is due to a giant underground supervolcano that is waking up. It had been considered dormant until ground temperatures began to rise in 2003, water began to boil, and volcanic gasses trapped underground began to be released. And in 2006, it was discovered that the land above this supervolcano was rising 10 centimeters per year.

You get the picture. Birth pains. Progression. All of this activity worldwide is leading to a climax of earthquake and volcanic activity that will occur during the tribulation period, as described in Revelation.

There are at least five massive earthquakes described in Revelation, one of which will level every mountain and sink every island (Revelation 16:18-20). We also find descriptions of smoke and sulfur pouring into the atmosphere, the sun being darkened, and bodies of water being poisoned—all language related to massive disasters of nature.

Famine and Epidemics

Following the logic and framework described above, we would expect to see famine increase in the period following WWI. In Luke's account of the disciples' end-time talk with Jesus, the writer includes pestilences, or disease, as a sign, along with famine.

At the end of WWI, the flu epidemic of 1918 took more lives worldwide than did the war. After the war, famine increased due to collapsed economies, industries, and logistical systems. What's surprising today, however, is that with all of our modern agriculture, GMOs, global export systems, and food preservation methods, there are still famines in various places around the globe.

If you were alive during the 1980s, you'll remember the famine in Ethiopia, during which more than 400,000 people died. Then there was the emergence of diseases such as AIDS, and, more recently, the Zika Virus. We have also seen outbreaks of diseases we thought were under control or eliminated, such as Ebola, cholera, and an absolute explosion of STDs. There has even been a recent outbreak of the bubonic plague (also known as black death) in Madagascar and several southeastern African countries. We're also finding that many diseases we thought were defeated are now showing resilience against antibiotics. And we are now facing a new crop of superbugs that have no known cure.

Likewise, famine currently grips much of the world due to climate conditions, disease, poverty, corruption, war, and refugee crises. My home church is involved in missions work in the Dominican Republic and Haiti, among other places, and I've seen famine firsthand. In Haiti, the children in a village we support eat once every other day and don't see this as a hardship. I've been to Brazil, where you can see mansions and then hundreds of poor street children living just a block or two away. There is no middle class in many such countries. You are either rich or impoverished.

Just recently the UN reported that there are 20 million people at risk of starvation and disease across four countries in Africa. It is reportedly the world's largest crisis since 1945.[6] This, on the heels of the terrible refugee crisis and famine conditions caused by the civil war in Syria.

Other Kinds of Natural Disasters

As I write this chapter, Texas is recovering from Hurricane Harvey, which dumped 11 trillion gallons, or 51 inches of rain, on Texas—an all-time record. Thirteen million people were under flood watches or warnings, and 58 Texas counties were declared disaster areas. To put those numbers in perspective, in 2015, South Carolina suffered a "once-in-1,000-year flood" with 4.4 trillion gallons of water.

On the heels of Harvey came Hurricanes Irma and Maria. Irma was the strongest Atlantic storm ever recorded up to that point and completely destroyed small islands in its path. Maria delivered a direct blow to Puerto Rico, destroying its electrical grid and knocking out power on the entire island.

Also in 2015, California experienced the worst wildfire season on record, with 10,125,149 acres burned. Then in October 2017, northern California experienced a massive outbreak of fires, completely destroying more than 7,000 buildings, killing 42 people, and costing more than one billion dollars in damages.[7] This broke the 2003 record of 2,830 structures destroyed. The 2017 event also caused the greatest loss of life from a single fire in California, surpassing the 1933 Los Angeles fire, which killed 29 people.

In recent years we've seen absolutely unprecedented flooding, wildfires, extreme hot and cold weather, record snowfalls, record-breaking tornados, landslides, sinkholes, mass animal die-offs, and hurricanes. Each year brings events that break previous records.

There are some who say that things are the same as they've always been, but we're just more aware of these events because of mass media and the Internet. That's simply not true. Consider this one statistic: There were almost 19 times as many worldwide natural disasters in 2000 (526) than there were in 1962 (28).[8] Since 2000, this

increase has continued with 700 natural disasters in 2016.[9] It is as if the entire Earth is experiencing the birth pains mentioned in Scripture.

God's Billboard

God, in his mercy, always warns people. He is not willing that anyone should be separated from him, and he never judges without graciously giving people time to repent. In every case in Scripture where God brought judgment, he first sent clear signs and his prophets to warn people. I believe that is what God is doing now with the signs of nature. They are his billboards to get our attention—to awaken us.

As you take a careful look at the signs of nature, you can see that they are clearly progressing like birth pains, just as Jesus described. With so much happening today, it's easy to become desensitized to one disaster after another—especially when it is on the other side of the world or the other side of the country. But when you prayerfully consider the facts, the warning about the increase in natural disasters is hard to ignore.

Let's shift gears a bit and move from these physical signs to the spiritual signs that point to the soon return of the Lord.

CHAPTER 16

The Spiritual Signs

This gospel of the kingdom shall be preached in the whole world as a testimony to all the nations, and then the end will come.

MATTHEW 24:14

Nor did they repent of their murders, their magic arts, their sexual immorality or their thefts.

REVELATION 9:21

When I moved to Georgia from the metro DC area, I was introduced to many new things that no one warned me about, such as fire ants, cow ants, armadillos, wild boars, and rattlesnakes. We live in a typical suburban neighborhood, yet I've had armadillos, opossums, a raccoon, and a skunk try to live under my back porch over the past ten years. I've become an expert small mammal trapper, and I have the number to animal control in my mobile phone contacts list.

There's another thing we were introduced to a couple years after we relocated to Georgia—microbursts. I assume they can happen anywhere, but I never experienced one until living in the South. A microburst is a sudden, powerful downdraft from a storm system. If you haven't witnessed one, it's like getting caught in a miniature hurricane with little to no warning.

Fortunately, our whole family was home at the time. From the preceding sights and sounds we thought a tornado was approaching, so we all went to a closet under the stairs in the middle of our house. After about two minutes the noise died down, so we emerged, and what we saw outside was unbelievable. Trees were down all over the neighborhood. Tree branches and debris covered our yard. At the park across from our house, younger trees were snapped in half 15 to 20 feet up from the ground, while several large and mature trees were ripped right out of the ground—flipped over with their giant root systems exposed. A several-mile-wide swath of our community was hit by the burst, and there was an amazing amount of damage. Fortunately for us, our house was damage-free and required only a bit of outdoor cleanup.

While this experience would have made a great introduction for the previous chapter because of the destructive nature of the storm, I mention it here to illustrate a key point about the spiritual signs we are told to watch for. During the microburst, we never saw the wind. Rather, we saw the *effects* of the wind. Also, the storm seemed to pop up out of nowhere, but it had been developing for some time. With spiritual signs, it's much the same. We can't see the spiritual realm, but if we view our world through the eyes of Bible prophecy, we can see the effects of end-time spiritual developments in our physical world.

The Bible gives us several spiritual signs to look out for as the end of the church age approaches. Some are subtle or hidden from the view of most, while others are like microbursts, tornados, or hurricanes. What is unique about this particular sign category is there are both positive and negative signs. To catch a breather, let's start with the positive signs.

The Positive Spiritual Signs
Gospel Preached to the Whole World

In Matthew 24:14 we read, "This gospel of the kingdom will be preached in the whole world as a testimony to all nations, and then the end will come."

Think about this statement for a moment. Jesus's dirty dozen (the 12 disciples) from this tiny area in the Mideast were tasked with sparking a movement that would reach every part of the globe. This movement spread out from there to the entire Roman Empire and beyond—reaching portions of the European continent, Asia, and north Africa within a few hundred years.

Fast-forward to the Great Awakening of the 1730s and 1740s, when iconic figures like George Whitfield and Jonathan Edwards preached to thousands at a time. This and other factors helped lead to the modern missionary movement of the late 1700s, which had the intent of fulfilling the great commission.

Matthew 28:19-20—Therefore go and make disciples of all nations, baptizing them in the name of the Father and of the Son and of the Holy Spirit, and teaching them to obey everything I have commanded you. And surely I am with you always, to the very end of the age.

Fast-forward again to the early- and mid-1900s, during which God used evangelists like the late Billy Graham as well as many Christian ministries to reach millions with the gospel. Billy Graham filled stadiums all over the world and used emerging satellite broadcasting technology to reach as many people as possible.

QUICK FACT: DID YOU KNOW...
that Billy Graham preached at 417 crusades in 185 countries on 6 continents and reached more than 210 million people?

Fast-forward again to our day, with the Internet now reaching almost every area of the globe. More than ever before, the gospel is going to the entire earth. There are still some people groups to which we have not yet presented the gospel or translated the Bible into their language. At a 2011 event in Orlando, Florida, organized by the Billy Graham Center at Wheaton College, it was stated that the Great Commission would be fulfilled by 2021–2026. By that time frame, every people group on earth will have heard the gospel and had some portion of Scripture translated into their language.

Revival in Darkest Places

While Christianity wanes in the West, for the first time ever, revival is exploding in some of the darkest, most oppressive countries on earth. In Iran, for example, thousands of Muslims are turning to Christ in response to Internet ministries and Christian programming on satellite television and over radio waves. There are also many reports of Muslims having dreams of Jesus reaching out to them. Elam Ministries estimates that there are more than 360,000 Christians in Iran. In 1979, there were only about 500.[10]

This phenomenon is occurring in many other parts of the Muslim world as well as in various Syrian refugee camps and intake locations. In a CBN article, best-selling author and prophecy expert Joel Rosenberg reported that "from 1960 to 2010 the number of Muslims that have converted to faith in Jesus Christ has grown from fewer than 200,000 to some 10 million people."[11]

Prophecy Unsealed

When God revealed visions about the future to Daniel, the prophet was perplexed and wanted to know what they all meant, particularly as they related to the end times. But he was told that his visions were to be sealed—mysteriously incomprehensible and out of reach—until the time of the end. We read this in Daniel 12:4, 8-9: "You, Daniel, shut up the words, and seal the book until the time of the end; many shall run to and fro, and knowledge shall increase...Although I heard, I did not understand. Then I said, 'My lord, what shall be the end of these things?' And he said, 'Go your way, Daniel, for the words are closed up and sealed till the time of the end'" (NKJV).

What Daniel 12:4 says about knowledge increasing in the time of the end likely has a dual application. Knowledge in general has absolutely exploded, as has the understanding of Bible prophecy. As the world stage continues to be set, prophecies that perplexed experts from a previous generation are now understood with clarity. The closer we get to the tribulation, the more we are able to understand about end-time prophecy. With each step toward the epicenter of activity, clarity grows and prophecies are unlocked—which is what we were told would happen according to the book of Daniel.

The Negative Signs
False Christs and Cults

There have always been small-scale false Christs, particularly in the early church and again as we draw closer to the tribulation period. During the 1800s, the number of cult groups ramped up broadly with the founding of Mormonism and the Jehovah's Witnesses, among others. Since then we've experienced a major explosion of cults around the world.

cult = a religion regarded as
noun   unorthodox or spurious.

The term *cult* is a fairly modern word with many applications. Most cults were started by a single leader. Some of these people claim to be prophets or messengers of God. Most cults grow out of Christian and Jewish roots, use Scripture selectively, and twist it or add to it. The evil forces behind cults know that a little bit of truth is needed to sell the lie.

This topic is obviously too broad to cover in a few paragraphs, but what's important to note is Jesus's prediction that the rise of false Christs would be among the birth pains that increase as the tribulation period draws closer. I also believe it is significant that the rise of modern-day cults has occurred during the same century that the Zionist movement for a Jewish homeland began.

PARTIAL LIST OF CULTS
Mormonism • Jehovah's Witnesses • Christian Science
Scientology • Unification Church • Branch Dividians
The Children of God • The People's Temple • Heaven's Gate

Apostasy

Christianity is losing its foundational stronghold upon the West, and secularism, cults, and occult influences are filling the void. Recent studies show that Christians are more biblically illiterate than ever, and many denominations now have a form of godliness but deny its real power (2 Timothy 3:5). A 2017 Barna study revealed that only 17 percent of professing Christians hold to a biblical worldview.[12] Harvard, Yale, and Princeton originally had Christian roots. Since 2001, more than 500 churches in London have been turned into private homes and mosques, while 423 new mosques have opened.[13]

Even in certain evangelical circles, apostasy is trying to metastasize. "Pastors" like Brian McLaren and authors like Rob Bell are persuading many that the fundamentals of the Christian faith are up for grabs. Teachings about biblical inerrancy and the reality of hell are cast aside while God's nature and God's grace are turned into anything one wants them to be.

> Matthew 24:10—At that time many will turn away from the faith and will betray and hate each other.

Those influences, along with other progressive postmodern ideas and sensibilities, are slowly creeping into evangelical circles and causing churches to water down—or completely redefine—the message of the gospel in order to appeal to a broader base. As each generation of Christians becomes less biblically literate, error is able to creep into the church with greater ease, frequency, and breadth.

The ultimate fulfillment of end-times apostasy will occur during the tribulation, when a one-world false religious system will be established in conjunction with the one-world government. We already see the groundwork for this being laid as various leaders advocate for an acceptance of all religions. This ecumenical unity sounds warm and appealing, but Scripture is clear that salvation comes only by the cross, and only to those who believe in Christ and accept his offer of forgiveness. Truth is not relative. Competing facts concerning salvation and eternity are mutually exclusive. Logic demands that they cannot all be true.

Not to pick on my Catholic friends, but one glaring example of this ecumenical spirit is seen in the positions of Pope Francis—one of the most prominent global spokespersons of our day. He has stated that all religions share the same God: "All of us together, Muslims, Hindus, Catholics, Copts, Evangelicals [Protestant] brothers and sisters—children of the same God—we want to live in peace, integrated."[14] He further stated that "all of us together, of different religions" are "children of the same Father."[15] Yet Jesus himself said, "I am the way and the truth and the life. No one comes to the Father except through me" (John 14:6).

Matthew 7:13-14—Enter through the narrow gate. For wide is the gate and broad is the road that leads to destruction, and many enter through it. But small is the gate and narrow the road that leads to life, and only a few find it.

2 Peter 3:9—The Lord is not slow in keeping his promise, as some understand slowness. Instead he is patient with you, not wanting anyone to perish, but everyone to come to repentance.

Persecution

The year 2015 was the worst in history for persecuted and martyred Christians, with an astounding 105,000 killed. That's twice as many as the previous year. And 2016 was not much better, with 90,000 Christians killed for their faith. That's an average of one death every six minutes.[16]

Matthew 24:9 —Then you will be handed over to be persecuted and put to death, and you will be hated by all nations because of me.

There has also been a significant resurgence of anti-Semitism in Europe, and that will only worsen as Muslim refugees continue to make up a larger proportion of the population on the European continent. Countries like Iran and groups such as Hezbollah continue to deny Israel's right to exist as they funnel terrorism her way, while the UN has long maintained a hostile posture toward Israel. Sadly, Israel's greatest historical ally, the United States, also turned its back on the Jewish nation during the Obama administration, creating the worst diplomatic relationship the US has had with Israel since the nation's birth in 1948.

On December 23, 2016, one day before the beginning of Hanukkah and two days before Christmas, UN Resolution 2334, which claimed Israel's settlements had no legal validity, passed due to America's refusal to use its veto power—something it has always done when anti-Semitism raised its ugly head in the UN. To make matters worse, on January 15, 2017, more than 70 nations gathered in Paris for an unprecedented global conference called the Paris Peace Conference. The purpose was to push heavily for a "two-state solution" in the hopes of attaining peace in the Middle East.

QUICK FACT: DID YOU KNOW...

Genesis chapter 10 lists the 70 patriarchal founders of the nations established after the flood of Noah's day?
The list of 70 nations is known as "The Table of Nations."

Genesis 10:32—These are the clans of Noah's sons, according to their lines of descent, within their nations. From these the nations spread out over the earth after the flood.

Another dangerous development for Israel was the Iranian nuclear "deal" arranged and supported by the Obama administration. This agreement puts Israel directly in harm's way by allowing Iran to continue developing its nuclear capabilities. On October 1, 2015, Israel's prime minister Benjamin Netanyahu stood before the UN General Assembly and delivered one of the most intense speeches I have ever seen. He pointed out that as Iran threatens to destroy Israel, the response from the international community has been "Utter silence. Deafening silence!" Then he gave the UN members a 45-second silent stare down, waiting to see if anyone would respond to his charge. No one did. These days, Israel increasingly stands alone in the world community, as predicted in Scripture.

Zechariah 12:3,6—On that day, when all the nations of the earth are gathered against her, I will make Jerusalem an immovable rock for all the nations. All who try to move it will injure themselves. ...On that day I will make the clans of Judah like a firepot in a woodpile, like a flaming torch among sheaves. They will consume all the surrounding peoples right and left, but Jerusalem will remain intact in her place.

Rise of the Occult

The book of Revelation reveals to us that occult practices will run rampant in the unbelieving world during the tribulation period, during which time the masses will be fooled by a great delusion. That being the case, we should expect to see the conditions for this beginning to form as we draw closer to the tribulation.

In recent decades we've seen occult and satanic influences spread far and wide. We've witnessed the proliferation of psychics, witchcraft, astrology, and other occult practices as they have become increasingly more prevalent and integrated into Western culture.

Entertainment is a reflection of culture. You want to know where a culture is headed? Take a look at its art and entertainment. Have you noticed that some Super Bowl halftime shows, prime-time music award ceremonies, concerts featuring various pop stars, and festival events like Tomorrowland or Burning Man have become increasingly dark, hypersexual, anti-Christian, man-centered, and bizarre?

"Art" exhibits by modern "artists" such as Marina Abramović reflect these attributes as well and employ overtly satanic rituals in their exhibits and art shows. Abramović claims not to be a satanist, but her occult practices—whether she knows it or not—are satanic. She is highly connected to Hollywood, New York, and Washington elites. So-called artists are given a pass for creativity and expression, and this has been used by the enemy to infuse pop-culture with occult practices and symbolism.

Strong Delusion

There are scores of other examples I could share concerning the rise of the occult, and this rise is related to another negative spiritual sign: a strong delusion. Do a bit of research yourself, and you'll find that these occult influences are growing across the globe, softening the battlefield for the great deception that will come as soon as millions of Christians disappear in the rapture.

Currently we don't see worldwide supernatural events, but the unbelieving world will need answers after the rapture happens. Satan has been preparing for that moment for two millennia, and as soon as the restraining influence of the church and the Holy Spirit are out of the way, hellish forces will break loose on earth with supernatural lying signs and wonders.

2 Thessalonians 2:9,11—The coming of the lawless one will be in accordance with how Satan works. He will use all sorts of displays of power through signs and wonders that serve the lie...For this reason God sends them a powerful delusion so that they will believe the lie.

So what is *the lie*, and how is the world being groomed for it today? Prophecy experts speculate about this, but there are indicators in Scripture and recent history that can guide us a bit. The *theory* of evolution is usually taught as absolute truth and has become the ingrained belief system of mainstream secular educational and scientific communities around the world. Alongside of that, the belief in alien beings from other worlds has also come to the fore. As we will see in a moment, these delusions are linked, and many prophecy experts believe they will influence the strong delusion that occurs during the tribulation.

In a lead-up to the deception—in whatever form it takes—culture is already beginning to adhere to upside-down ideas. For example, in some political circles, climate change is seen as a greater danger than Islamic terrorism. Transgenderism is pushed on our children and into their bathrooms and locker rooms. Israel is seen as an oppressor rather than a small peaceful democracy surrounded by hostile terrorist enemies. Modern-day champions of the feminist movement have become staunch defenders of Islam, which oppresses women's rights in horrific ways. These current delusions show how the world is being conditioned to accept illogical ideas en masse prior to the tribulation period. More and more, logic and common sense are being thrown out the window.

Isaiah 5:20—Woe to those who call evil good and good evil, who put darkness for light and light for darkness, who put bitter for sweet and sweet for bitter.

Scoffers

While in college, I interned as a graphic artist for the Department of the Interior in Washington, DC. One day a coworker in our office was listening to a famous shock jock on the radio. I have forgotten what the topic was, but this radio personality started belittling the Christian belief that Jesus was coming back. He thought Christians were weak-minded, brainwashed idiots because it had been almost 2,000 years since Jesus was on earth, yet they still believed Jesus would return one day. He said something along the lines of, "Face it. Your Jesus is not coming back. He was not the Savior of the world. He was just a man."

Then this shock jock used that as a basis to mock other foundational aspects of Christianity, such as the resurrection and Jesus's sacrificial death for our sins. His comments were in passing, but they stood out to me because I had just recently heard a sermon on 2 Peter 3:3-4, which states, "Above all, you must understand that in the last days scoffers will come, scoffing and following their own evil desires. They will say, 'Where is this "coming" he promised?'" This famous shock jock had both components: He scoffed at the idea of Christ's return, and he was well known for celebrating and highlighting extreme immorality and anything irreverent, shocking, or vulgar. This is just one example of how our world is increasingly mocking Christianity.

Two Sides, Same Coin

The positive and negative spiritual signs are two sides of the same coin. Both will be on full display all through the tribulation. As we draw near to the Lord's return, our God, who is full of mercy and grace, will extend every opportunity for people to trust in him before the rapture. Likewise, as Satan sees the same signs we do, he will do everything in his power to keep people from turning to the only One who can save them.

These spiritual trends will reach their apex during the tribulation period. Revelation informs us that occult practice and demonic activity will be prevalent around the world. At the same time, 144,000 Jewish evangelists will be boldly proclaiming the gospel all over the globe, and vast numbers of people will choose to follow Christ and will become thoroughly committed to him—many to the point of martyrdom.

The gloves will be off. There will be no pretense. Nothing will be subtle or covert. Again, both sides of the spiritual coin will be on full and ultimate display. Even now, as we look around us, we're beginning to see the spiritual conditions of the tribulation cast their shadows before their full arrival.

CHAPTER 17

The Signs of Culture

Mark this: There will be terrible times in the last days. People will be lovers of themselves, lovers of money, boastful, proud, abusive, disobedient to their parents, ungrateful, unholy, without love, unforgiving, slanderous, without self-control, brutal, not lovers of the good, treacherous, rash, conceited, lovers of pleasure rather than lovers of God.

2 TIMOTHY 3:1-4

Several years ago, I was selected to be on a grand jury. Every Friday for six weeks I had to report to the Prince George's County Courthouse in Upper Marlboro, Maryland. I thought I would be put on a single case the whole time, but I received a real-world civics lesson as I learned the process. Rather than serve on a single case, we reviewed 40-60 cases each week to see if there was enough evidence for them to go to trial.

I had always assumed that whatever crimes and court cases we heard on the local news provided a clear snapshot of the most egregious crimes in our area. Boy, was I wrong. Week after week, we reviewed horrific cases of murder, attempted murder, child abuse, pedophilia, witness intimidation, domestic violence, and the like—all of which I would have expected to be on the news.

Each week we also heard from various law enforcement officers who would provide insight into what they saw on a daily basis. Most of us live without much thought about crime unless it invades our lives. But, police, firefighters, EMTs, and other public servants see a side of life very different from what most of us know.

Listening to the experiences of these public servants helped me understand the current reality of our society. If we take out the distracting fluff about who's going to be in the next season of *Dancing with the Stars*, which Hollywood couple is about to break up, or what gossip is about to come to light concerning the rich and famous, we find that the daily news headlines that really matter are, well, scary and depressing—unless you understand Bible prophecy.[17]

SNAPSHOT OF THE INCREASE OF VIOLENCE

TYPE OF VIOLENCE	DATE(S)	LOSS OF LIFE
Mexican Drug War	2006 to present	120,000+ and 27,000+ missing
Abortions in the US	1973 to present	59,745,450 and counting
Terrorist Attacks	2017 up to 12/1	1,054 attacks 7,294 fatalities on every continent except Antarctica

An Increasingly Corrupt and Violent Society

Before Paul wrote 2 Timothy, Jesus provided similar information about society during his Olivet Discourse. He stated that just before his return, conditions would be like those in the days of Noah and Lot. In Luke 17:26, 28-30 he said, "Just as it was in the days of Noah, so also will it be in the days of the Son of Man...It was the same in the days of Lot. People were eating and drinking, buying and selling, planting and building. But the day Lot left Sodom, fire and sulfur rained down from heaven and destroyed them all. It will be just like this on the day the Son of Man is revealed."

In the Days of Noah and Lot

It's worth taking the time to interpret scripture with scripture, so let's see what we can learn from Genesis about the days of Noah and Lot. This will help shed light on what Jesus was talking about. Consider the following verses:

Noah

> Genesis 6:11—"Now the earth was *corrupt* in God's sight and was full of *violence*" (emphasis mine).

> Genesis 6:13—"So God said to Noah, 'I am going to put an end to all people, for the earth is filled with violence because of them. I am surely going to destroy both them and the earth.'"

Lot

> Genesis 18:20-21—"The LORD said, 'The outcry against Sodom and Gomorrah is so great and *their sin so grievous* that I will go down and see if what they have done is as bad as the outcry that has reached me. If not, I will know'" (emphasis mine).

The events that followed, and Lot's response to them, both point to just how violent and immoral society had become. Please excuse the graphic nature of the content, but Scripture does not shy away from telling it like it was.

> Genesis 19:4-8—"Before they had gone to bed, all the men from every part of the city of Sodom—both young and old—surrounded the house. They called to Lot, 'Where are the men who came to you tonight? Bring them out to us so that we can have sex with them.' Lot went outside to meet them and shut the door behind him and said, 'No, my friends. Don't do this wicked thing. Look, I have two daughters who have never slept with a man. Let me bring them out to you, and you can do what you like with them. But don't do anything to these men, for they have come under the protection of my roof.'"

In Our Current Day

The days leading up to the flood and the destruction of Sodom and Gomorrah were characterized by violence, murder, lawlessness, and extreme sexual immorality. Sound like our day? Consider these telling statistics about violence: During the entire decade of the 1980s there were 46 riots worldwide. In 2011 alone, there were 106.[18] In 2017, the US experienced the deadliest mass shooting to date, with 58 people killed and more than 515 wounded in Las Vegas.[19] This broke the previous year's record of 49 killed and 58 wounded in an Orlando nightclub. Ten years ago, a mass shooting on this scale would have dominated the news for weeks. Now they are so common that within a few days of the event there's barely any further mention of the tragedy.

As for immorality, consider these statistics from 2016: Just one major pornography site reported that 23 billion visitors watched 4.6 billion hours and 91,980,225,000 videos, and that it had an average of 64 million people watching per day. Those are the statistics of just one site. There are about 428 million other sites.[20]

QUICK FACT: DID YOU KNOW...

That 1 in 10 pornography sites are visited by children under 10 years old?

Source: http://www.mirror.co.uk/tech/one-10-visitors-porn-sites-8868796

Basic decency, civility, and long-honored values continue to slide off the moral cliff with increasing speed as people become more narcissistic and self-centered. Key Hollywood, media, political, and sports figures continue to face the music as scandal after scandal reveals patterns of widespread, systemic sexual abuse in these industries.

Leaders who were once seen as role models are dropping like proverbial flies as their immoral behavior catches up with them. They include some of the biggest names and the offenses they have committed have become more and more disturbing, including horrific sexual abuse and pedophilia.

The character and morality of man has so declined that every single end-time characteristic described in 2 Timothy 3 is manifest in our day. Where there is no boundary, the flood of destructive immorality will continue to overflow the banks of God's protection.

As these banks overflow, we see other negative results as people pursue pleasure with no regard to consequences. For example, since 1999, drug overdose deaths in the US have increased from 18,000 or so per year to more than 64,000 in 2016, with no sign of slowing down.[21]

At the same time, the numbers of those afflicted by sexually transmitted diseases (STD) have hit an all-time high. With immorality celebrated in all its various forms, there has been an absolute explosion of STDs in the past decade. In 2016 there were two million new reported cases (an all-time high). and 2017 continued on the same trajectory.[22]

Jesus also informed us in Matthew 24:12 of this fact: "Because of the increase of wickedness, the love of most will grow cold." What immediately comes to mind when I read that verse are the video clips that showed abortion industry executives casually talking about selling aborted baby parts for as much money as they could get. When governments around the world sanction and even promote the taking of innocent life in the womb, the love of many has indeed grown cold.

How Did We Get Here?

In Romans, Paul explained the progression of lawlessness that occurs when people reject God and his ways. Romans 1:18-32 describes the downward spiral of judgment that occurs when a person or country continues to reject God and the principles revealed in Scripture. It's a lengthy passage, but worth citing here, as it relates to what conditions will be like as we approach the end times.

> The wrath of God is being revealed from heaven against all the godlessness and wickedness of people, who suppress the truth by their wickedness, since *what may be known about God is plain* to them, because God has made it plain to them. For since the creation of

the world God's invisible qualities—*his eternal power and divine nature—have been clearly seen,* being understood from what has been made, so that people are without excuse.

For although they knew God, they neither glorified him as God nor gave thanks to him, but their thinking became futile and their foolish hearts were darkened. *Although they claimed to be wise, they became fools* and exchanged the glory of the immortal God for images made to look like a mortal human being and birds and animals and reptiles.

Therefore *God gave them over* in the sinful desires of their hearts to sexual impurity for the degrading of their bodies with one another. *They exchanged the truth about God for a lie,* and worshiped and served created things rather than the Creator—who is forever praised. Amen.

Because of this, *God gave them over to shameful lusts.* Even their women exchanged natural sexual relations for unnatural ones. In the same way the men also abandoned natural relations with women and were inflamed with lust for one another. Men committed shameful acts with other men, and received in themselves the due penalty for their error.

Furthermore, just as they did not think it worthwhile to retain the knowledge of God, *so God gave them over to a depraved mind,* so that they do what ought not to be done. *They have become filled with every kind of wickedness, evil, greed and depravity.* They are full of *envy, murder, strife, deceit and malice.* They are *gossips, slanderers, God-haters, insolent, arrogant and boastful; they invent ways of doing evil; they disobey their parents; they have no understanding, no fidelity, no love, no mercy.* Although they know God's righteous decree that those who do such things deserve death, they not only *continue to do these very things but also approve of those who practice them* (emphasis mine).

In the formerly Christian West, we've seen this Romans 1 progression toward moral and sexual debauchery play out to the point that today, we're witnessing a fully depraved cultural mindset on all fronts. If there is no creator, there is no accountability. If we are here by random chance, there can be no laws that govern our behavior. Ultimately, anything goes in a world dominated by the survival of the fittest. No God equals no morality—no right and wrong.

One note here, and please let me be clear: God loves even the worst of sinners. In Luke 19:10, we read that "the Son of Man came to seek and save the lost." This refers to all unbelievers, including those who are engaged in the worst forms of immorality or who are confused or misled about their sexual identity. We all need God's grace, forgiveness, restoration, and healing. As sinners, none of us is better than any other person. Your sins and mine put Jesus on the cross just as much as the sins of those who are hardened criminals and murderers.

Christians need to consistently reach out to unbelievers in genuine love and build relationships that allow them to make known the life-changing message of Christ. These people need to hear the truth that all sin, including our own, is rebellion against God that can be changed by the healing love and forgiveness of Christ. We must also warn of coming judgment. As in the days of Noah, God's gift of forgiveness and safety is a limited-time offer.

Isaiah 55:6-7—Seek the Lord while he may be found; call on him while he is near.

That said, it seems as if the downward spiral described in Romans 1:18-32 is occurring globally at an unprecedented pace. Scan the headlines of various news outlets for a few minutes, and it becomes undeniable that violence and immorality are increasing exponentially all around the world. Yes, there has always been violence and immorality, but not to the level or extent which we see today.

The Natural Conclusion of Lawlessness

Violence and immorality are now the norm. For anyone who stops to think about it, it's clear we're living in days eerily similar to the times of Noah and Lot, just before God's judgment fell. Again, a rubber band can be stretched only so far before it breaks. Likewise, the cup of God's wrath, described in Revelation, will eventually reach a tipping point. God will not let wickedness go on indefinitely. A day of reckoning will come.

CHAPTER 18

The Signs of Technology

*You, Daniel, shut up the words,
and seal the book until the time of the end;
many shall run to and fro, and
knowledge shall increase.*

DANIEL 12:4 (NKJV)

Like most kids, my love for animation started at an early age. I was a child of the seventies and early eighties—the days of Saturday morning cartoons, 2D animated cereal commercials, and set times for specific cartoons to air.

You couldn't watch cartoons whenever you wanted to. No smart phones. No Netflix. No Internet. Just you, a TV with a handful of channels, an 8-10:30 a.m. block of your favorite Saturday morning cartoons, and a bowl of your favorite cereal. Mixed in with Scooby Doo, the Smurfs, He-Man and the Masters of the Universe, and School House Rock were some older cartoons from the sixties, like The Flintstones and The Jetsons.

The Jetsons was an early sixties animated series produced by Hanna-Barbera featuring a futuristic family that made use of amazing technological gadgets such as a phone watch, a house-cleaning robot, flying cars, and an automated kitchen. Many of these once-imagined technologies are now a reality for us.

The Terminator. Robocop. Minority Report. The Matrix. As with The Jetsons, these blockbuster movies have several things in common, not the least of which is the futuristic technology inherent to their storylines. It's interesting to observe how future tech portrayed in cartoons like The Jetsons or movies such as *The*

Terminator, Robocop, or *Minority Report* eventually becomes reality. Human imagination drives technological advancements. We live in a day in which the breakneck speed of technology development is hard to keep up with—and makes the fulfillment of end-time prophecies more and more possible.

There's an often-overlooked relationship between technology and prophecy. Many predictions in Scripture require some kind of advanced technology to be available before an event can occur. The prophets of old simply delivered the messages and visions they received from the Lord, and usually didn't understand much about the prophecies themselves. Many of the prophecies they proclaimed could not have been fulfilled at the time they were given.

Nuclear weaponry, satellite and Internet broadcasting, massive data centers, DNA manipulation, artificial intelligence, surveillance systems, and many other current and emerging technologies are either described in Bible prophecy or are logically necessary for end-time events to occur. With everything that we've learned in previous chapters, let's look now at this category of end-time signs.

The Main Tech Sign

In Daniel 12:4 we gain critical insight into a key end-time sign. An angelic messenger delivered a message to Daniel and had just finished describing end-time events, including details about the tribulation period. Then the messenger told

Daniel that these prophecies would be sealed, locked, or hidden from understanding until the time of the end, when travel and knowledge would increase.

In other words, the prophecies in Daniel would not make much sense for most of history. But as the end of the age approached, they would be unsealed. This unsealing would occur simultaneous with great technological advances in travel and human knowledge. With that in mind, consider these facts.

Less than 200 years ago, the fastest way to travel was on horseback. We didn't fly until December 14, 1903, when Orville Wright successfully flew for a whopping 12 seconds. Since then we've broken the sound barrier, been to the moon and back, set up an international space station, and made worldwide travel easily accessible to just about anyone.

I can jump on a commercial passenger plane in Atlanta, and literally be on the other side of the world in less than 17 hours. The US Air Force's X-15, the fastest manned aircraft ever, can travel 4,520 mph, or 6.72 times the speed of sound. The X-15 is capable of beating my commercial airline trip by about 14.5 hours, flying to the other side of Earth in about 2.5 hours.

Earlier in this book we learned that until the early 1900s, human knowledge doubled about every century. By the end of WWII, knowledge doubled every 25 years. Today there are so many forms of new knowledge that we can't keep up.

In addition to general human knowledge, many prophecy experts point out that Daniel 12:4 also means that end-times prophecies will be unlocked in the last days. This means that many prophetic passages that were unable to be understood in the past are being unlocked in our generation, resulting in greatly increased prophetic knowledge as we study the Scriptures and consider current events.

With the fulfillment of prophecy concerning the super sign of Israel becoming a nation again, many prophecy students have once again embraced a literal interpretation of Scripture. During this same time period (since 1897, when Theodor Herzl organized the first Zionist Congress), travel and knowledge have exploded. That is no coincidence.

THEODOR HERZL
1860–1904

Gospel Tech

In chapter 16, as we looked at the spiritual signs connected to the last days, I highlighted Matthew 24:14, which informs us that the end of the age would come once the gospel was proclaimed to the whole world. Without rehashing the spiritual aspects of the sign, I'd like to highlight the technological aspect.

When the first-century church began, there were a few hundred believers in Judea, and the only way to share the gospel to the masses was by speaking to crowds that were within hearing distance of one's voice. But by the second half of the twentieth century, evangelists such as Billy Graham could use radio, television, film, live broadcasts of stadium events, and any other emerging technology that allowed them to spread the gospel. Today we have access to the Internet, satellite TV, and other advanced technology that can help us to proclaim the gospel to every area on earth.

BILLY GRAHAM

Even in remote areas where there is no Internet, tech companies are developing drone networks that will be able to be used in places where cell towers and satellite receptors are not available. A few years ago, on a mission trip to a remote area of the Dominican Republic, I was surprised to find an Internet café where locals lined up to take turns on a handful of Internet-connected computers in order to check their Facebook pages and do online searchs.

> Matthew 24:14—This gospel of the Kingdom will be preached in the whole world as a testimony to all nations, and then the end will come.

The first 24-hour news channel was CNN, founded in 1980. Since then 24-hour news has become the norm and we've added multiple ways to stay connected to live news, including push notifications on our phones, live Internet streaming, and even news screens at gas pumps! The Internet, satellite broadcasting, and other interconnected technologies make certain prophecies possible for the first time in history—not the least of which is the capability to broadcast the gospel to anywhere in the world.

Beast Tech

In Revelation 13 we learn about a technological system that will be used by the antichrist and the false prophet during the tribulation period. Somehow they will be able to force the people of the world to receive some type of mark on their right hand or forehead. Only those who have this mark will be able to buy and sell goods, and they cannot receive the mark unless they worship the antichrist.

> Revelation 13:16–17—It also forced all people, great and small, rich and poor, free and slave, to receive a mark on their right hands or on their foreheads, so that they could not buy or sell unless they had the mark, which is the name of the beast or the number of its name.

At minimum, this mark system will require four types of technology to be available: a global cashless system, massive data storage facilities, superprocessing capabilities, and some type of device that connects each individual to this system. In chapter 14 we looked at the societal push toward a one-world cashless currency. What we're talking about here is the technology needed to make it a reality, along with a system capable of tracking billions of people.

We see from Revelation 13:16-17 that only those who have the mark will be able to buy and sell. The world monetary system will be integrated with mark-of-the-beast technology—whatever that winds up being. Right now, there are several candidates already available: RFID (radio-frequency identification) chips, digital tattoos, and even less invasive technologies like facial recognition software, eye scans, and the like.

QUICK FACT: DID YOU KNOW...

that pictures tagged on Facebook reside in databases with facial recognition technology and that Facebook has many new facial recognition patents pending?

Perhaps the final version of this mark technology will be a combination of all of the above and more. My point is, all these technologies exist right now. Massive data storage centers with the capacity to store data well beyond current levels have been constructed in recent years, and additional facilities are planned or already under construction. For example, the NSA opened a $1.5 billion, one-million-square-feet data center in Utah. Google reports having at least 15 data centers around the world. Facebook has at least four international data centers in use and three more under construction.[23]

Today's supercomputers can process data at unbelievable speeds. For example, IBM's Watson can process at a rate of 80 teraflops. If you are like me, that doesn't mean much. More simply, that means the supercomputer can handle 80 trillion operations per second. The ability to process a massive amount of data global system quickly and efficiently is already here.[24]

Nuclear Tech

The writers of Scripture had no frame of reference for nuclear warfare and therefore no words to describe it in terms we are familiar with. Instead, they simply described what they saw in their prophetic visions. With that in mind, consider these verses, which may be describing nuclear warfare.

Revelation 8:7—"*A third of the earth was burned up*, a third of the trees were burned up, and all the green grass was burned up" (emphasis mine).

Revelation 6:4—"Another horse came out, *a fiery red one. Its rider was given power to take peace from the earth* and to make people kill each other. To him was given a large sword" (emphasis mine).

Zechariah 14:12—"This is the plague with which the LORD will strike all the nations that fought against Jerusalem: *Their flesh will rot while they are still standing on their feet*, their eyes will rot in their sockets, and their tongues will rot in their mouths" (emphasis mine).

But one of the most telling passages in Scripture about what seems to be nuclear war is found in Ezekiel 38–39 regarding the war of Gog and Magog.

In Ezekiel's description of this end-time battle that will most likely occur early in the tribulation period or just before, we find some curious language that lines up with a description of nuclear warfare. In addition to a massive earthquake, we are told God will bring a sword against Gog (the title of the leader of the enemies).

One phenomenon this sword will bring is burning sulfur from the sky (38:22). Then we learn in 39:9-10 that after Israel's miraculous victory, the enemy's weapons will be used for fuel for seven years. Many experts believe this could refer to Israel converting nuclear weapons into usable nuclear fuel.

We also find a few other curious statements in the Ezekiel passage. In 39:12-16, we read about a two-phase cleanup process that will include professionals who dispose of bodies. In the immediate phase, these professionals will bury any corpse they find. In the second phase, they will "carry out a more detailed search" for any bones that are left (verse 14). They will leave a marker by the bone, then other professionals will relocate the bones to a downwind valley. These details seem to describe the cleanup of radioactive contamination after nuclear warfare.

New Frontier Tech

There are also many emerging technologies that will surely enhance and heighten what I've mentioned above. The recent advances in artificial intelligence (AI) have even made tech leaders like Elon Musk (Tesla, SpaceX) nervous. Vladimir Putin told a group of students on September 1, 2017 that the one who achieves a breakthrough in the AI sphere will dominate the world.

In 2017, Andy Levandowski, a self-driving car engineer and cofounder of Otto (an autonomous trucking company), started a new religion that worships artificial intelligence. This new religion is called Way of the Future. Official nonprofit papers were filed in May 2017, and the goal of their activities are to focus on "the realization, acceptance, and worship of a Godhead based on Artificial Intelligence (AI) developed through computer hardware and software."[25]

Revelation informs us about an image of the beast that will seem to come to life. People will be instructed by the false prophet to make an image of the beast, and evidently this image will be given life, the power to speak, and the power to cause people to be killed (see Revelation 13:14; 14:9-11; 15:2; 16:2; 19:20; 20:4).

The way the text is worded, it's not clear whether mankind collectively is instructed to create one single image of the beast, or if every person is to make an image. Experts differ on this, but the prospect of each person or each household having their own image is frightening—it's a lot like the way idol worship took place in ancient times.

Perhaps a technology will be developed that allows each person or each household to create an image of the beast that is connected to the beast system. It's clear in Scripture that worshipping the beast, worshipping his image, and receiving his mark will be a package deal.

I don't know if the image of the beast will be a CG-driven hologram or something physical that can be touched, but among the more amazing aspects of this image are its capability to speak and reason, and to have nonworshippers killed wherever they may live. One of the current fears about AI's ability, if applied, is autonomous weaponry. Future battlefields will consist of drone robots that are manually or autonomously controlled. This technology will surely be used by the beast system to enforce worship. Suddenly, the dystopian backstory of the movie *The Terminator* doesn't seem so farfetched.

I'LL BE BACK.

Technology and God's Timing

Sci-fi eventually meets reality. It's here, and it was predicted for the end times. Aside from the aforementioned technology, God could fulfill every prophecy strictly on a supernatural basis, but if we consider God's past pattern of action, we should expect prophecy to be fulfilled in the midst of real-world technological developments. Indeed, the technologies required for the last days to take place are very much at hand.

CHAPTER 19

The Sign of Convergence

Even so, when you see all these things, you know that it is near, right at the door.

MATTHEW 24:33

One of my favorite animated films is Pixar's 2004 movie *The Incredibles*. In it there is a scene where Helen Parr (aka Elastigirl) is flying a jet to reach her husband Bob (aka Mr. Incredible) on a mysterious unknown island. Just as she discovers that two of her children snuck aboard the jet, she learns that it is being pursued by multiple heat-seeking missiles.

After attempting evasive maneuvers and calling out Mayday signals on the radio, it becomes clear to Helen that no one is coming to their aid, and whoever launched the missiles is not calling them off. The missiles hone in on the jet, tracking with its speed, and they begin to converge from all sides. Just before they make impact and destroy the jet, Helen's daughter Violet forms a force field around the three passengers and saves their lives while the jet explodes around them, raining down fiery debris.

Using that scene as an analogy to explain the convergence of end-time signs, the missiles represent various signs that have come into view. If the launch of the first missile represents the roots of Israel's rebirth at the 1897 Zionist Congress, then the final shot in the scene, where all of the missiles begin to converge, would represent where we are today. For the first time ever, all of the major signs and sign categories are in play. There is nothing that we can point to that must occur before the seven-year tribulation takes place except the rapture of the church, and then the confirming of a covenant or treaty by the antichrist. We know from Scripture that the former must occur before the latter. In other words, the rapture could happen at any time, and the stage is set for all future end-time events to occur.

With regard to timing, many a prophecy teacher has used the analogy of the holiday season in America. If we see Christmas decorations going up, we know Thanksgiving is near. Likewise, when we see tribulation-period conditions forming, we know the rapture is near, for it must precede the tribulation.

Like two bookends of the signs categories we've been reviewing, Israel and convergence frame the discussion. On one end, we have the rebirth of Israel. This super sign clearly set the end-time clock into motion. On the other end we have all the signs converging simultaneously.

Many prophecy experts have noted that prophetic developments have increased significantly over the past decade. And have you noticed our culture's recent obsession with apocalyptic themes and storylines? It seems every few months a new TV show, movie, or video game with some type of an end-of-the-world scenario is released. Why is this? Could it be that we intuitively know that history is heading toward a conclusion?

If you and I believe Scripture, then we can't ignore the fact that Jesus instructed us to look for the convergence of the end-time signs, which will indicate that his return will happen very soon. In Luke 21:28, Jesus said, "When these things *begin* to take place, stand up and lift up your heads, because your redemption is drawing near" (emphasis mine).

A Snapshot of Today

I'm hesitant to list the convergence of signs occurring at the time of the writing of this chapter because they are occurring at such a fast pace that I'm afraid such a list will quickly become out of date!

Isaiah 11:11 tells us that Israel would be born in a day, and that the birth pains would begin *after* birth. Amazingly, this is exactly what we see happening in our day. Do we see the rise of Russia and a Russian-led Arab coalition, an increase in travel and knowledge? Have we seen world war followed by massive disease and famine, worldwide earthquakes, increased persecution of Christians and Jews, and a growing apostasy in churches? Have we seen increased lawlessness and violence, moral decline, and numbers of scoffers? Have we seen movement toward a one-world currency, government, and religion? Have we seen the emergence of the technology required for end-time events to occur? Do we see these signs increasing in frequency and intensity after Israel became a nation again? Yes. All these things are clearly converging in our day.

Add to all of that the fact that the United States of America—the wealthiest, most powerful Gentile nation on earth, known for being the melting pot of the world—is more divided than it has been since the 1960s or possibly even the Civil War. Political strife is at an all-time high.

We're also in debt to the point that it's pretty much impossible to ever repay our obligations. The US national debt was under $2 trillion in 1985, but at the time of this writing it is well over $20 trillion and climbing rapidly. If you want get your anxiety up, just log onto USDebtClock.org and watch your blood pressure climb with the US national debt. What's true for people is true for countries: You can get into so much debt that there's no way out, and all it takes is one crisis to cause everything to collapse.

Couple that with the fact that as a nation we have made it the law of the land that God is not allowed in schools, that abortion is legal, and that the God-ordained institution of traditional marriage is no longer sacred. And we wonder why families and communities are falling apart. In the words of Billy Graham's wife Ruth, "If God doesn't judge America, He'll have to apologize to Sodom and Gomorrah."[26] (Source: https://billygraham.org/story/billy-graham-my-heart-aches-for-america/.)

In the Ezekiel 38–39 war of Gog and Magog, we see that "Tarshish and her villages" will do nothing more than merely protest the attack on Israel. Some prophecy experts agree that "Tarshish and her villages" is a reference to England, America, and other countries like America that were once colonies of England. If that is the case, during the war of Gog and Magog, neither England nor America will come to Israel's aid. It seems that by that point, America will be in a weakened state and will not be able to help.

If the Lord's return is close, as it seems to be, could it be that the rapture and the chaos that ensues is what tips the scales of America's collapse? I think that is very likely.

Stay Alert!

The missiles are converging. The Christmas decorations are going up. A rubber band can be stretched only so far. Birth pains can continue for only so long. Something has got to give. Sooner or later, the proverbial baby must be born. We seem to be nearing that point. I opened this chapter with Matthew 24:33, which informs us that when we see these things, we know Jesus's return is near—right at the door.

Isaiah 66:9—"Do I bring to the moment of birth and not give delivery?" says the Lord. "Do I close up the womb when I bring to delivery?" says your God.

It seems that it is time for us to be more alert! We dare not attempt to set a date or a time frame, but it is biblical for us to look for and know the season of His return—and it seems we are closer to that season than many people realize.

Scripture is clear that no man knows the day or the hour (Matthew 24:36; Mark 13:32). But we are expected to know the season of His return (Luke 12:56; Hebrews 10:25). The closer His return appears, the stronger our desire should be to live for Him, and the more boldly we should share our faith!

This book is structured in such a way that it builds to what is stated in this chapter. If you happened to jump right into this chapter without reading the preceding ones, I would encourage you to go back and read them, as they lay a necessary foundation for the conclusions you've read here. Also, what I've highlighted here can be overwhelming and a bit scary to ponder. That's why I encourage you to continue on to the next chapter and learn about the safest place to be in these dangerous times.

CHAPTER 20

The Safest Place to Be (in Christ)

The Lord is not slow in keeping his promise, as some understand slowness. Instead he is patient with you, not wanting anyone to perish, but everyone to come to repentance.

2 PETER 3:9-10

The first mission trip I ever went on was to Brazil. Our goals were to build a two-story orphanage and to tell people about Jesus at nightly open-air evangelism meetings in villages, schools, and various areas of a city called Belo Horizonte. Some of the places we planned to go to were in rough, undeveloped areas, and a few people from our team expressed their fears about this.

The missionary who was organizing the team and our stateside logistics had been to Brazil several times on mission trips, and he shared some great wisdom with us about the fear we were all experiencing to one degree or another. He said, "There is no safer place than at the center of God's will." We all talked about that principle a bit, and it was both encouraging and sobering. He didn't say, "God is going to keep you perfectly safe and unharmed." His point was that as long as we were doing what we knew God had called us to do, ultimately, nothing else mattered.

Your Next Step: A Starting Point

The church where my family and I serve developed a process for identifying practical ways for believers to grow spiritually. It's called Next Steps. The idea is that no matter where you are in the process of knowing Jesus, everyone has a next step. It's sort of a spiritual GPS. Jesus's parting instructions for Christians was to "go and make disciples" until the end of the age. Discipleship, or spiritual growth, occurs one step at a time.

With a deeper understanding of Bible prophecy and its implications for us today, what should be our next step? Where do we go from here? Well, it depends on where you are. If the safest place to be is at the center of God's will, what is the first step to being in God's will?

The Safest Place to Be

When it comes to the last days, you may wonder if there's really any safety from the chaos to come. We're not immune to the events of the world, but there is ultimately a safe place to be regardless of what is going on all around us or even to us. If you haven't already, I want to invite you to make an all-important first step—accepting Jesus's gift of salvation to begin a personal relationship with him today. The safest place to be is not a place, but a person. Step one to being in God's will is to be *in Christ*.

Romans 8:1—Therefore, there is now no condemnation for those who are in Christ Jesus.

I can't assume you know Christ just because you are reading a book about Bible prophecy. Perhaps you've been around Christian culture just enough to inoculate you to it. There is a world of difference between knowing *about* Jesus and *knowing* Jesus. I don't want to miss an opportunity to lay it out as clearly as I can.

If you have read this far but don't know him, something has intrigued you enough to hold your attention. Someone is drawing you. That someone is the Holy Spirit. Perhaps you don't fully understand how all this works (join the club), and you have doubts and questions. That's okay. You don't have to know everything to believe in something. We tend to say, "Show me and I'll believe," but God says, "Believe, then I'll show you." It's a paradox, like many other aspects of theology and faith.

If you are honest with yourself, you'll admit you mess up. You do things wrong. You're not an axe murderer, but from time to time you break even your own rules. Again, join the club. We are an imperfect people. We inherited a sin nature from our ancient ancestors, Adam and Eve. They were created sinless and lived in an unfallen paradise in close communion with God. But something happened.

Satan, a fallen angel who was originally one of God's greatest created beings, tempted Adam and Eve to rebel against their Creator by eating of the fruit of the tree of the knowledge of good and evil—the only thing that was off limits to them in Eden. They fell for the bait, and the law of sin and death took effect. Sin entered God's creation, bringing death and decay.

This fallen nature was passed down to all of us like an inherited trait from our ancient ancestors. Sin is in our DNA, so to speak. It's part of who we are. We're not sinners because we sin. We sin because we're sinners. We're not let off the hook though, because we each practice sin. We have all knowingly chosen to do the wrong things at times. We are sinners by nature and by practice.

Our sin has separated us from a holy and pure God. Like oil and water, sin and holiness do not mix. So we have a problem. God can't overlook sin. No matter what we do, we can't work or will our way to God. The separation is too great.

But where there was a problem, God brought a solution. In his unbelievably great mercy, he sent his sinless Son to pay our sin debt in full. Your sins and mine were hung on the cross. The Creator of the universe zipped on some skin and became one of us. Somehow he was fully God and yet fully man. He faced every temptation you or I would ever have—and then some—yet lived a sinless life.

This sinless life, foreshadowed by the spotless lambs sacrificed under the Old Testament law, was our substitute. Isaiah said that God "laid on him the iniquity of us all" (Isaiah 53:6). We were in debt beyond repair. All of our proverbial credit cards were maxed out, and the payment needed far outweighed our ability to even put a dent in it. But Jesus took our debt for us. He made possible a new beginning. A second chance. A fresh start.

But there's one thing left to complete the transaction. God is a gentleman and never kicks down the door to your free will. A forced gift is no gift at all. We all must make a choice at some point. Will we choose to accept the gift? Or will we leave it there, weighing down the outstretched hands of the grace-filled Gift Giver?

In Revelation 3:20, Jesus said, "Here I am! I stand at the door and knock. If anyone hears my voice and opens the door, I will come in and eat with that person, and they with me." God is relational. Personal. He's not cold and distant. But, it's up to you. Relationships are a two-way street. If you haven't already, you need to make a choice. Will you open that door? Will you accept the gift? Will you begin a relationship with the Savior? You can do it right now.

If you have never accepted the Lord's gift of salvation, now is the time. I plead with you to ask Jesus to be your Savior. It's not a matter of how good you are; it's a matter of how good he is. He took all your sin on him at the cross. You can't *be* good enough. Only he can. He died as your substitute. He took the rap for you—but you must place your faith in him.

> Romans 5:8—God demonstrates his own love for us in this: While we were still sinners, Christ died for us.

This is not a scare tactic, but I truly believe time is short. The converging signs point to a soon-returning King and an even sooner rapture. Even if I'm wrong, we are not guaranteed our next breath. If accepting Christ is something you want to do, here's how. It's very simple, but people often make it too complex. One does not become a Christian by following a formula, but I've found that what I'm about to share is an effective way to explain what it means to receive Christ and become a true Christian. It's so simple a child can understand it. It's as simple as A, B, C.

Admit that you are a sinner. None of us are perfect. We all fall short. Romans 3:23: "All have sinned and fall short of the glory of God." Romans 6:23: "The wages [payment] of sin is death, but the gift of God is eternal life in Christ Jesus our Lord."

Believe that Jesus is God's Son and that he died on the cross with your sins on him. Romans 5:8: "While we were still sinners, Christ died for us."

Confess him as your Lord. This doesn't mean you will never mess up again. Rather, it means you will serve him and learn his ways as you grow spiritually. Romans 10:9: "If you confess with your mouth the Lord Jesus and believe in your heart that God has raised Him from the dead, you will be saved."

"Lord Jesus, I admit that I am a sinner. I have sinned against you, and sin separates me from you. I thank you that you died on the cross for me. You took my sins upon you and paid my penalty at the cross. I believe you are who you say you are—God in the flesh. I believe you died for my sins. I want to accept your gift of salvation and, at this moment, I ask you to be my Savior. I thank you for this great forgiveness. I now have new life. I now claim you as my Savior and my Lord. In Jesus's name, amen."

On page 214 is a simple prayer you can pray. These words aren't magic. Again, this is not a formula. But if these words accurately reflect the motives of your heart, then when you pray this prayer you will become a Christian. You will have placed your faith in Christ and will have had your sins forgiven. You will look forward to an eternity with Jesus in heaven, and you will avoid the terrible time of tribulation that will soon come to the world. Pray this prayer now.

If you just prayed that prayer, you are a new creation. The Bible tells us that heaven is celebrating right now because of your decision. The Holy Spirit now indwells you and will guide you and keep you. You won't be perfect, but you are forgiven, and he will never leave you. His work in you has just begun. You are an adopted coheir with Christ. You will one day live and reign with him in the millennial kingdom and forever in eternity. Welcome to the family of God!

If you have not accepted Christ because you have doubts, questions, or reservations, that's okay, but don't leave them there. Please investigate them fully. Also, I dare you to pray this prayer: "God, if you are the God of the Bible and Jesus is the Son of God, please open my eyes and help me believe. I want to know truth wherever it may lead."

If the Bible is just a book of fairy tales to help people cope with life and God is not real, then you just prayed to the air. But if he is real and your prayer for finding truth was sincere, I believe you are in for an interesting journey. Keep praying that prayer, and watch what happens.

John 14:6—Jesus answered, "I am the way and the truth and the life."

Now that we've established that having a relationship with Christ is the starting point, what's next? How should we live in these very interesting times? Turn the page, and let's find out!

CHAPTER 21

How Should We Live?

*The night is nearly over; the day is almost here.
So let us put aside the deeds of darkness
and put on the armor of light. Let us behave
decently, as in the daytime, not in carousing
and drunkenness, not in sexual immorality and
debauchery, not in dissension and jealousy.
Rather, clothe yourselves with the Lord
Jesus Christ, and do not think about
how to gratify the desires of the flesh.*

ROMANS 13:12-14

I train at a local gym run by the coach of the USA kickboxing team. One day during a sparring session, I had gone a few rounds and began to slow down a bit midway through the last round. Like any good trainer, my coach started pushing me. "Don't stop pressuring. Use your speed," he said. Through my mouthpiece I replied, "I'm gassing out." Then my coach—knowing that fighters can push themselves beyond their perceived limits—said, "You can be tired later. Finish strong."

That advice resonated. In boxing and kickboxing, you train to fight in explosive bursts, and even when exhausted you have to maintain an active rest. You never stop moving. You never allow your opponent to know when you are tired. There's a saying we use at the gym: "Train hard. Fight easy." That speaks volumes. If you push yourself when you don't have to, you'll be ready to push yourself when you really need to. If you prepare now for the big moment, you'll be glad you did.

You may be growing weary as you look at the world around you. But the signs of the times tell us it's almost the end of the fight. In this final chapter I want to address how we ought to live. All that we've studied about Bible prophecy should count where the rubber meets the road. The culmination of this book should affect our behavior—to lead us to practical real-world action. Don't gas out now! Keep pushing until the final bell has rung.

> Philippians 3:13-14—Forgetting what is behind and straining toward what is ahead, I press on toward the goal to win the prize for which God has called me heavenward in Christ Jesus.

The verse at the beginning of this chapter links the knowledge of Christ's soon return with behavioral choices and a dedication to Christ that is reflected in our daily lives. Scripture is clear that we can't know the day or hour of his return, but hypothetically speaking, if you knew Jesus was coming in the next hour, would you rejoice, or would you feel regret and anxiety? It depends on how you are living.

Bad Stuff Out

The first step in getting to the safest way to act is to get rid of known, habitual sin. Talk to another believer you trust. Repent and confess your sin to God in prayer. Become accountable. Apply Scripture to your struggle. Plug in to a local group of believers if you aren't involved in a church. That community will help you grow and help you resist "the sin that so easily entangles us" (Hebrews 12:1). Get anything out of your life that needs to be out. Anything you give up for Christ is always replaced by something better. Don't believe the lies of the enemy that say otherwise, and don't stop fighting. Even if you get knocked down 100 times, get back up each time. Never give up.

> Hebrews 12:1—Therefore, since we are surrounded by such a great cloud of witnesses, let us throw off everything that hinders and the sin that so easily entangles. And let us run with perseverance the race marked out for us.

Good Stuff In

As we allow the nearness of Christ's return to drive us to get the bad stuff out of our lives, we should also allow it to motivate us to get the good stuff in. We need to study God's Word like the Bereans did. They searched the Scriptures daily (Acts 17:11). We need to do that while we watch for the signs of his return. We also need to serve others in the name of Christ—to live selflessly and generously. We need to tell other people about Christ by building meaningful relationships with them and finding ways to point them to our Savior. We need to mentor, teach, and disciple new believers.

> Galatians 6:9—Let us not become weary in doing good, for at the proper time we will reap a harvest if we do not give up.

A key way to bring good stuff in is to assemble together regularly. In this day of online everything, it's easy to remain isolated and detached from other believers. Yet community is important. If at all possible, we need to be regularly involved in a real and physical local body of believers.

> Hebrews 10:25—...not giving up meeting together, as some are in the habit of doing, but encouraging one another—and all the more as you see the Day approaching.

Finally, we need to stay united. I'm sad to say, I've seen way too many Christians wasting time and energy attacking each other about secondary issues and church traditions. Please resist this. Let the world see your love for your Christian brothers and sisters—even when you disagree with them. Don't divide over minor issues. Rally around Christ and the fundamentals of the faith, not your pet theology or passion.

It seems that the enemy is working overtime to cause division, especially among those who study Bible prophecy. A house divided can't stand. There's room for debate, but not for hate. We need to redirect that sideways energy to things that matter, like telling people about our Savior.

> John 13:35—By this everyone will know that you are my disciples, if you love one another.

Parting Words

At the very end of the book of Revelation, Jesus said, "Behold, *I am coming quickly, and My reward is with Me,* to give to every one *according to his work.* I am the Alpha and the Omega, the Beginning and the End, the First and the Last" (22:12-13 NKJV, emphasis mine).

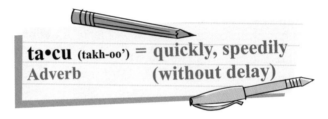

ta•cu (takh-oo') = **quickly, speedily**
Adverb   **(without delay)**

He's coming quickly. Once end-time events are in motion they will occur in rapid-fire succession. The 2,000+ years of waiting will end abruptly as events quickly take place beginning with the rapture. The church, known as the bride of Christ, will be whisked away and given her rewards.

> 2 Corinthians 5:10—For we must all appear before the judgment seat of Christ, so that each of us may receive what is due us for the things done while in the body, whether good or bad.

One of those rewards is the crown of righteousness. Paul wrote in 2 Timothy 4:8, "Now there is in store for me the *crown of righteousness,* which the Lord, the righteous Judge, will award to me on that day—*and not only to me, but also to all who have longed for his appearing*" (emphasis mine).

Did you catch that? Those who long for his return will receive a special reward. The Bible lists several other crowns and other potential rewards. It also gives us insight that these are eternal rewards—which means they will stay with us. Apparently even the laying of our crowns at Jesus's feet (Revelation 4:10) is not a one-time opportunity. Like rank insignia in the military, or the well-earned scars of a warrior, our rewards will stick with us and be celebrated by others because of the glory they bring to the Savior. That's worth getting excited about.

If you are like me, you have been wounded. You have fought some battles. You have had some hard things occur in your life. You have failed at times and had to turn to the Lord for forgiveness. You have persevered through times of loneliness, despair, and hardship. Guess what: You are a victorious overcomer. The Lord knows every detail of what has happened to you, and when you see him face-to-face, it will all make sense.

My prayer is that this book will help us gain spiritual eyes to see, spiritual ears to hear, a quickening heartbeat as we watch for his return, and courage to give it everything we've got until the final bell has rung!

Habakkuk 2:3—For the revelation awaits an appointed time; it speaks of the end and will not prove false. Though it linger, wait for it; it will certainly come and will not delay.

NOTES

1. Tim LaHaye and Jerry Jenkins, *Are We Living in the End Times?* (Carol Stream, IL: Tyndale, 2011), p. 304.

2. Lee Strobel, *The Case for Christ* (Grand Rapids, MI: Zondervan, 1998); *The Case for Faith* (Grand Rapids, MI: Zondervan, 2000); *The Case for a Creator* (Grand Rapids, MI: Zondervan, 2004).

3. Lee Strobel, *The Case for Christ* (Grand Rapids, MI: Zondervan, 1998), p. 183.

4. This statement comes from the German Lutheran theologian Rupertus Meldenius, and was written in a tract written about Christian unity circa 1627.

5. Patrice Lewis, "Is Knowledge Doubling—or Halving? *WND*, May 27, 2016, https://www.google.com/amp/mobile.wnd.com/2016/05/is-knowledge-doubling-or-halving/amp/; David Russell Schilling, "Knowledge Doubling Every 12 Months, Soon to Be Every 12 Hours," *Industry Tap*, April 19, 2013, http://www.industrytap.com/knowledge-doubling-every-12-months-soon-to-be-every-12-hours/3950.

6. Faith Karimi, "20 million at risk of starvation in world's largest crisis since 1945, UN says," CNN, March 12, 2017, http://www.cnn.com/2017/03/11/africa/un-famine-starvation-aid/index.html.

7. "The Latest: Official: California fire losses top $1 billion," October 19, 2017, http://www.foxnews.com/us/2017/10/19/latest-california-mountain-fire-threatens-300-homes.html.

8. Max Roser and Hannah Ritchie, "Natural Catastrophes, Our World in Data," https://ourworldindata.org/natural-catastrophes.

9. "Weather-related disasters are increasing," *The Economist*, August 29, 2017, https://www.economist.com/blogs/graphicdetail/2017/08/daily-chart-19).

10. "Muslims Turning to Christ Across the Middle East," CBN News, January 12, 2017, http://www1.cbn.com/cbnnews/cwn/2017/january/muslims-turning-to-christ-across-the-middle-east.

11. Emily Jones, "Seeking Revival in the Muslim World," June 8, 2016, https://www1.cbn.com/cbnnews/world/2016/june/seeking-revival-in-the-muslim-world; "Thousands of Muslims reportedly turning to Christ in Middle East," Fox News, January 11, 2017, http://www.foxnews.com/world/2017/01/11/thousands-muslims-reportedly-turning-to-christ-in-middle-east.html; Rebecca Flood, "Christian Conversion: Wave of Muslims in Middle East turning to Christ after violence," Express, January 10, 2017, http://www.express.co.uk/news/world/752551/Muslim-Christian-convert-Islam-church-Iran-Europe-religion.

12. "Competing Worldviews Influence Today's Christians," Barna, May 9, 2017, https://www.barna.com/research/competing-worldviews-influence-todays-christians/.

13. Stoyan Zaimov, "500 UK Churches Closed While 423 Mosques Were Built on 'Sad Ruins of English Christianity,'" *The Christian Post*, April 3, 2017, https://www.christianpost.com/news/500-uk-churches-closed-while-423-mosques-were-built-on-sad-ruins-of-english-christianity-report-179320/.

14. Elahe Izadi, "Pope Francis washes the feet of Muslim migrants, says we are 'children of the same God,'" *Washington Post*, March 25, 2016, https://www.washingtonpost.com/news/worldviews/wp/2016/03/25/children-of-the-same-god-pope-francis-washes-the-feet-of-muslim-migrants/?utm_term=.c652d2f33485.

15. Izadi, "Pope Francis washes the feet of Muslim migrants."

16. Perry Chiaramonte, "Christians the most persecuted group in world for second year: Study," *Fox News,* January 6, 2017, http://www.foxnews.com/world/2017/01/06/christians-most-persecuted-group-in-world-for -second-year-study.html.

17. "The Rise of the Urban War Correspondent on Twitter," MIT Technology Review, July 16, 2015, https://www .technologyreview.com/s/539406/the-rise-of-the-urban-war-correspondent-on-twitter/; see also http://www .numberofabortions.com https://storymaps.esri.com/stories/terrorist-attacks/?year=2017.

18. "List of riots," Wikipedia, https://en.wikipedia.org/wiki/List_of_riots.

19. "Deadliest Mass Shootings in Modern US History Fast Facts," CNN, February 19, 2018, https://www.cnn .com/2013/09/16/us/20-deadliest-mass-shootings-in-u-s-history-fast-facts/index.html.

20. "World's Largest Porn Site Reveals the Most-Searched Porn Genre of 2016...," Fight the New Drug, January 9, 2017; "Porn Stats: Which Country Produces and Hosts the Most Porn?" Fight the New Drug, November 22, 2017, https://fightthenewdrug.org/most-popular-porn-genre-search-of-2016/; and https:// fightthenewdrug.org/porn-stats-which-country-hosts-most-porn/.

21. "Overdose Death Rates," National Institute on Drug Abuse, September 2017, https://www.drugabuse.gov/ related-topics/trends-statistics/overdose-death-rates.

22. Sandee LaMotte, "New STD cases hit record high in US, CDC says," CNN, September 28, 2017, http://www.cnn.com/2017/09/26/health/std-highest-ever-reported-cdc/index.html; "STDs hit all-time high in U.S.," *Chicago Tribune*, September 27, 2017, http://www.chicagotribune.com/lifestyles/health/sc -hlth-stds-all-time-high-1004-story.html.

23. Domestic Surveillance Directorate, NSA.gov, https://nsa.gov1.info/utah-data-center/; Google Data Centers, https://www.google.com/about/datacenters/inside/locations/index.html; Dave Smith, "Take a look at Facebook's gorgeous data centers from around the world," *Business Insider*, February 16, 2017, http://www .businessinsider.com/facebook-data-centers-photos-2017-2/#heres-a-look-inside-facebooks-data-center-in -forest-city-north-carolina-the-company-launched-this-center-in-2010-1.

24. "IBM Watson supercomputer," WhatIs.com, http://whatis.techtarget.com/definition/IBM-Watson-super computer; IBM, https://www.ibm.com/watson.

25. Mark Harris, "Inside the First Church of Artificial Intelligence," *Wired*, November 15, 2017, https:// www.wired.com/story/anthony-levandowski-artificial-intelligence-religion/; Summer Meza, "Religion that Worships Artificial Intelligence Wants Machines to Be in Charge of the Planet," November 17, 2017, http:// www.newsweek.com/google-executive-forms-religion-artificial-intelligence-714416; John Brandon, "An AI god will emerge by 2042 and write its own bible. Will you worship it?" *Venture Beat*, October 2, 2017, https:// venturebeat.com/2017/10/02/an-ai-god-will-emerge-by-2042-and-write-its-own-bible-will-you-worship-it/.

26. Billy Graham, "My Heart Aches for America," Billy Graham Evangelistic Association, July 19, 2012, https://billygraham.org/story/billy-graham-my-heart-aches-for-america/.